VIJAY NAMBISAN (1963-2017) was a poet, writer of non-fiction, critic, journalist and translator. He won the first All India Poetry Competition (organized by the Poetry Society of India and the British Council) in 1990 with his poem 'Madras Central', and his debut collection, *Gemini*—a shared edition with Jeet Thayil, and introduced by Dom Moraes—was published two years later. His second collection, *First Infinities*, appeared in 2015. In between, he published two acclaimed non-fiction books, *Bihar Is in the Eye of the Beholder* (2000) and *Language as an Ethic* (2003), as well as *Two Measures of Bhakti* (2009), comprising translations of the devotional poetry of Poonthanam and Melpathur Narayana Bhattathiri.

Vijay Nambisan was married to the novelist and surgeon Kavery Nambisan, with whom he spent several years in rural and small-town Tamil Nadu, Bihar, Maharashtra and Karnataka.

PRAISE FOR VIJAY NAMBISAN

'Hell, or a state very much like it, does feature in Nambisan's poetic underworld, which is deep, intricate and enticing. But its attendant horrors are never indulged in for their own sake and are kept well in check by a certain wit, a muscularity of mind, which remind me of a similar grace in poets as far distant in time from each other as Robert Graves and John Donne.'

—Adil Jussawalla

'Nambisan's view of humankind is bleak, his view of the possibilities of poetry even bleaker. The Gods are lonely and turned away by "the mobs…at every border", and no amount of poetry can breathe life into a dying city. We have art so that we may not perish by the truth, Nietzsche says, and Nambisan's art is of the highest order, a reminder of what English-language poetry in India can do when the language is handled with skill and passion by someone who is so clearly in love with it, in all its moods, from sombre to playful, from dark to light. This love is on display in every page of *First Infinities*, whose every line is worthy of his great precursors—"Arun and Dom and Nissim"—whom Nambisan so lovingly invokes in the book's opening poem.'

—Arvind Krishna Mehrotra

'Vijay Nambisan's sensuous, intelligent, and often unsettling poems are parables for the time we live in now, without in any way being portentous or just topical. Nambisan appears to achieve his mix of reporter's sense of being present at an important event of moment with the artist's refracted relationship with meaning through his preoccupation with formal design and mythic allusion. In poems such as "Millenium", whose "There was not much light in the world when we left" reworks Nissim Ezekiel's "Enterprise" ("It started as a pilgrimage"), Nambisan, half a century later, seems to extend and interrogate, while doggedly continuing with, the curious business of Indian poetry in English itself.'

—Amit Chaudhuri

These Were My Homes

Collected **POEMS**

Vijay
Nambisan

SPEAKING
TIGER

SPEAKING TIGER PUBLISHING PVT. LTD
4381/4, Ansari Road, Daryaganj
New Delhi 110002

Published by Speaking Tiger in hardback 2018

Copyright © Kavery Nambisan 2018

Introduction copyright © Rukmini Bhaya Nair 2018

ISBN: 978-93-88070-38-6
eISBN: 978-93-88070-37-9

10 9 8 7 6 5 4 3 2 1

Typeset in Goudy Old Style by Jojy Philip, New Delhi
Printed at Sanat Printers, Kundli

All rights reserved.
No part of this publication may be reproduced, transmitted, or stored in a retrieval system, in any form or by any means, electronic, mechanical, photocopying, recording or otherwise, without the prior permission of the publisher.

This book is sold subject to the condition that it shall not, by way of trade or otherwise, be lent, resold, hired out, or otherwise circulated, without the publisher's prior consent, in any form of binding or cover other than that in which it is published.

Contents

Introduction 11

GEMINI I

The Miracle of the Pomegranate	31
Reflections on May Day	32
Madras Central	33
paranoia/paranoia	35
Cats Have No Language	36
The Attic	37
Diary of the Expedition	39
Grandfather's Beard	43
Death of a Terrorist	44
Ill Met by Moonlight	45
The Garden Variety Show	47
Poetic Licence	49
Auto Da Fé	50
After Six Drinks	52
Drums at Night	53
Holy, Holy	54
Flotsam	55
Biography	56

Narcissus in the Drought   57

FIRST INFINITIES

Loss
- Dirge   61
- Words from the Dying City Came   63
- Ducks   63
- The Hole in the Earth   65
- Kalki   65
- Millennium   66
- Diogenes   67
- Elizabeth Oomanchery   68
- Aswatthama   69
- Snow   70
- Age Speaks to Age   71
- Christ Stopped Here   72
- Chyavana   76
- The Deserted Temple   77
- To HST   78
- Something Rich and Strange   79
- Medical Entry   80
- Mind the Gap   81
- Nila in Flood Time   82

Balance
- To the Lord of the Dance   87
- Spider   88
- Ilyushin   89
- De Maupussant's Lover   90
- Lady with Parrot   90

Bhima in the Forest	91
When Suddenly the Poems Die	92
The Door	93
The Nuns	94
To Have Been Written in Urdu	96
Śankuntala	97
Mahaśivaratri	98
Grown-up	98
To K, Who Said a Poem Ended Weakly	99
First Infinities: Need	100
First Infinities: Hospital	100
First Infinities: Drying Out	101
Dvija	102
You, Wystan Auden	109
To Dom	111
Half-life	112
Profit	
A Little Better	114
Essay in Capitalism	115
No Fallacy Is Pathetic	116
Meeting a Translator	117
The Fly in the Ointment	117
Names	119
Making Tea	120
Pills	120
Making Coffee	121
Lint	122
Those Blind from Birth	123
These Were My Homes	123
Wet Dream	124

On First Looking into Whitman's Humour	125
Summer Triangle	126
The Rain Is Pouring down Again	127
A Gift of Tongues	127
Neighbours	129
The Corporate Poet	130
A Town Like Ali's	132
Shame and Renown	133

NEW POEMS

Good Friday	137
Billennium	139
The Sunday Mystery Show	141
To Vivekananda, Jr	142
Schrödinger's Cat	145
The Temple	146
Lent	147
Cophetua	148
For the Tibetan New Year	149
The Evidence of My Senses	
Just Talk	150
Integument	151
Hear, Hear	151
Smell of Things to Come	152
An Eye for an Eye	153
All Cock	154

Familial
    One Gift My Father Gave Me   155
    My Father's Hand   156
    My Mother Would Not   156
    On Vishu   157
    Frost in Summer   158
Calypso to Odysseus   159
Duck Poems
    Buoyancy   160
    Original Sin   160
    Double Bill   161
    Mach Duck   161
    L'après-midi d'un Canard   162
Shanghai Girls   163
The Shopping Mall   165
Hand   166
Morning Walk   167

Introduction

The very first poem in this volume is 'The Miracle of the Pomegranate'. 'In the August rain,' it says, 'the flowers are changing / The shape of the tree.' Exactly twenty-five years after the publication of this poem in 1992, Vijay Nambisan passed away in August, raising once again that unanswerable but always haunting question about the relationship between poetry and prophesy.

What does a poet see that others cannot? In Vijay's intelligent, self-aware meditations on mortality and human folly in this final and complete volume of his poems, readers will come to as close an apprehension of the nature of epiphany as is possible—to those sudden illuminations of the spirit that can, without warning, light up flares in our dull, corporeal bodies. In Vijay's words, 'some stoves are born to make trouble / But this one clicks sweetly into flame'. Poetry is that space where words click, sometimes miraculously, into flame. Vijay knew this space most intimately; he was as familiar with it as the process of making coffee.

> I measure decoction into a cup,
> Add milk and water, pour the whole into
> A suitable cauldron, and place it
> On the stove...
>
> There is something in the making of coffee
> That dulls the moral sense.
>   I spoon in sugar

> And sip that first sip against which it is vain
> To argue.
> > Not strong enough.
> > > I must add
> Some instant powder, which I loathe, or spoon in
> Some more decoction, which will make it cold.
>
> This is not how the masters advocate
> The making of coffee, but I have succeeded
> In taking seven thinking minutes off my life.

Is this not an almost perfect description, impressively deadpan, of the process of producing that verbal decoction we call poetry? Further, in its implicit rejection of any predictable mastery over the process, its meditation on 'the moral sense', its Zen-like suggestion that the purpose of life is to bypass the toils of thought, is it not also akin to something like the prophet's vision?

The word 'prophesy' came into English from the Greek in the usual complicated fashion via Latin and French. A prophet was one who had 'the gift of interpreting the will of the gods'. True, it does appear improbable that Vijay would tamely agree on his elevation to prophetic status in the originary, old-fashioned sense of this 14th-century English word. Afterall, the 111 poems in this slender volume written over his brief lifetime lay no claim to a superior connection with any gods or demons. They display, instead, a keen understanding of science and its uncompromising rationality ('radium decays a little bit at a time'), of the temporary bonds of love and desire, of waddling ducks and arching cats, of the particular genealogies of speech that Vijay came to inherit through his father, his grandparents, his mother and aunts, and of the questing history of our bipedal species ('Diary of the Expedition'). This seems a set of concerns robustly tied to experiences of the then, here and now. Science, genealogy, observations of nature and animals, a record of passing moments of human contact, marked sometimes by playfulness but never by solemnity. Exactly where in these familiar themes lies the space for prophesy, that leaping desire to express the will of divinity? By what miracle does it happen?

Fine poetry, though, does not yield up its secrets easily. We find our first clue to Vijay's gift of looking into the heart of things, his seer's vision, in the recurrent themes of his poems ('The Deserted Temple', 'Christ Stopped Here', 'Good Friday') and in his obsessive rendering of mythological themes ('Aswatthama', 'Chyavana', 'The Lord of the Dance'). In 'Holy, Holy', he speaks of rain that 'threatens this ordinary day / With magic.'

Things that grow manifest,
Plainly, the unnatural: more sure
And permanent is the unwalked way,
Lifeless air, stone unencumbered
With feelings; not obsessed, therefore pure.

This talk of the 'unwalked way' glimpsed in rain-washed purity, of a world unsullied by human feeling, is not unrelated to saintly yearnings. Like so many of us today, Vijay confesses to being 'Born without a language and in the frightened iconoclasm of my age...I have burdened words with a soul whose sins are my own.' The prophet's business is to attend keenly to the voices that will lead us out of the wilderness of human suffering. It is exactly such an awareness of the high stakes involved that Vijay evinces in a poem like 'Narcissus in the Drought'.

> The stream sounds in my ears,
>   with a voice both clear and hoarse.
> There is flood in the air; in the mouth, great thirst,
> A prayer to the shadow to move a little more
> Towards a vision I know possessed me there before.

And then, at the end of this same poem, there is that clear-eyed, startling turn to personal extinction that seals the prophet's own fate, as Vijay declares without sentiment:

> I cannot hope to live now; but first
> It must hurt somewhat, to perish, not knowing why.

Poets like Vijay see as distinctly as any prophet what he calls 'The Hole in the Earth', the bog beneath our feet into which anyone of us can sink. It is this unusual 'prophetic' quality that makes his voice so valuable in our godless, techie times when each of us so easily has the chance to be a (false?) prophet on airy social media, to trade glibly in infinite futures. We must not forget, either, that the one book that Vijay ever translated was called *Puntanam and Melpattur: Two Measures of Bhakti* (2009), and there is little doubt that a kind of modernist 'bhakti' permeates Vijay's work when read in its entirety, even if it is not exactly a sanitized version of the emotion. 'There is a hole,' he writes, 'through to the earth's bowels.'

> I glimpsed it yesterday, outside the gate,
> A view of voided ground yielding voiceless vowels,
> Saying without speaking; and through what ways
> Winding, through what beatitude, what hate,
> What hope of sanctity

If 'something survives / The carrion bleaching of our lives', gives us the courage to look down at that hole and find in it future 'hope of sanctity' it is, in Vijay's book, the irrepressible form of language called poetry, as he emphasizes in his elegiac poem 'You, Wystan Auden'. Many readers of this volume will know that W.H. Auden's own elegy on the death of W.B. Yeats is one of the most enduring pieces of literature in the world, so there's a definite double entendre here. Poetry does not decay, it is distilled, disembodied thought and the surest pathway to immortality in the secular imagination, thus commandeering today some of the hoary functions of prophesy. This could be one reason why Vijay is so emphatic in his expectation of what a poem should be, and in his candid estimate of the sorts of people whom poetry leaves cold.

> I would like my poem to be
> Like my grandfather's beard, to be airy
> In the lean wind, to look up at the clouds
> And laugh. There are people unaffected
> By poetry, and there are those whom poetry
> Disregards—I would like to write a poem
> Like grandfather's beard.

It is possible that a sort of prophetic warning against disregarding and being disregarded by poetry at one's peril is being issued here—a theme reiterated in several other poems, such as 'Poetic Licence'.

> When my grandfather grew to be an old man,
> he was a little mad:
>   his hair turned black again
> and his voice held its own, and his eyes
> asked incessantly for answer, an answer...

> For my grandfather was once a poet
>   and some of the world's weight
> had lain upon his shoulders.

In short, 'long-recessive genes / are pressed into service' in Vijay's poems about his family, a family that is both a source of genealogical self-knowledge ('the world's weight') and of sardonic self and other criticism. He speaks frankly, for instance, without a trace of middle-class embarrassment, of his alcoholic's crazy capacity to grow maudlin.

> After Six Drinks
>
> I am grieving for everything which has occurred...
>
> I am willing my heart to beat faster and faster,
> Finishing life quickly. This is no ordinary ache.
>
> I am pouring my sorrow into a little cup,
> Just to drown the gods in—a libation, nothing more,
> And when we are being happy and the roof is on the floor
> Someone can reach out and casually drink me up.

As for comments on his fellow poets, Vijay is unsparing but not entirely without empathy for poor souls afflicted by the lethal virus of poetry. Read the lovely, tripping 'Elizabeth Oomanchery' or the punning 'On First Looking into Whitman's Humour' to encounter these delights. The self-referential irony displayed in 'The Corporate Poet' is equally illustrative. Vijay mockingly allows the speaker, a false claimant to poetic insight, to savage his own book, *Language as an Ethic*.

He will fashion a poem short, clever, pithy
For tomorrow's meeting with fifty college girls
Who'll find him remarkably urbane and witty.

If FA fails there's always the oration
On Language as an Ethic, from the Akademi's fête
He can render that without preparation.

Among the many things that can be 'rendered without preparation' is death, oftentimes shockingly. Fact is, one simply does not expect one's friends to die, especially a fighting spirit such as Vijay. Yet, as I have suggested in this essay, if one reads them posthumously, one unexpectedly finds in them acute anticipation, prophesies even, of their imminent demise. In this sense, mine is not, cannot be, a conventional introduction to a volume of poetry in the present case. Rather, it is that contradictory thing, at once an act of celebration and of mourning. For this reason, I include below, as a sharp incision in the uneven fabric of my introduction, the essay I wrote in August 2017, on first learning of Vijay's death.

In Memorium

FIRST INFINITIES

Last night, Vijay Nambisan startled me into wakefulness at 3.38 a.m., the time fast edging towards four in the morning. Sylvia Plath called it that 'still, blue, almost eternal hour' which produced poems for the ear rather that the eye. Unable to sleep on this oppressive August night, I stumbled towards my computer and began hesitantly to type: *all morning / on the feathered grass / the old peahen and I / mourning.* Then, I stalled. I had no idea whom or what I was mourning. It was at this point that my husband, sleepless too, came and announced: 'You know, Vijay Nambisan is dead.'

Coincidence, doubtless, but Carl Jung, it is reported, once presciently called coincidence the joker in nature's pack of cards. Vijay always had a quirky sense of humour. This, I believe, was his last tease, informing me that he was the subject of my poem, master of my halting words and the most exacting of language mavens.

Vijay took language as seriously as he took life. Language was his dangerous elixir. For him, language was no mere tool of communication; it embodied, rather, the art of survival. It was about everyday usage (the colloquial preference for the borrowed word 'machis' instead of the haute Hindi 'diyasalayi' in Bihar, to offer one of Vijay's own examples) but it was also about infinities of meaning, about all varieties of verbal enchainment and enchantment.

This fascination with language was a bond we shared. In the late 1990s and early 2000s, I met Vijay several times. He was on a roll, making his mark by winning the first All India Poetry Prize. Our books of poetry were published, one after the other, by David Davidar at Penguin. I don't think we realized just how lucky we were. Poetry seemed to matter then, as did experimental writing. Vijay could be extravagantly generous when it came to such daft ventures. When I published *Technobrat* in 1997, he gave it one of the most perceptive reviews the book received, declaring with his usual metaphoric felicity: 'Dr Nair wandered into [the IIT] system as a missionary might into the jungle. Getting a bunch of savage technologists, hungry for the red meat of practical solutions and contemptuous of the tenuous cartilaginous links of language, interested in even their own culture required the patience and skills of a Jane Goodall. I wish I had a course like HU484 when I was at IIT Madras and a teacher like Dr Nair.'

Vijay knew what he was talking about—he was that socially elevated person, an IIT graduate. No student ever 'wandered' into the IIT system; they got there by fighting the hard fight. I would have been so incredibly honoured to even come close to being Vijay's teacher. As it happened, it was more that I trailed after him, getting the All India Poetry Prize a year after he won it with the haunting 'Madras Central', entering the 'IIT system' as a teacher in the Humanities Department far more tamely than he did as a student blasting through all those tough competitive exams. Yet Vijay never bothered to claim his degree. That was the essential Vijay, smart and contrary as they come, fed on something far rarer than the 'red meat of practical solutions'. *For he on honeydew hath fed, and drunk the milk of Paradise.* Vijay showed the world what an 'IIT engineer' could be at his best—a thinker who belonged to the vanguard of the imagination.

Once, in the early days, the Sahitya Akademi organized a conference in Delhi where Vijay's thoughts caused a minor storm. He defended the virtues of writing in English. Years later, he elaborated this argument in print when he took on U.R. Ananthamurthy on the *bhashas* in the pages of *The Hindu*. They were both friends. I could not decide whose side I was on. Vijay had no such problems. He was not fussed about others' pettifogging opinions. On that Sahitya Akademi occasion, after all the righteous outrage, we escaped to the Lodi gardens. Parakeets wheeled overhead; broken blue tiles on stone. Peace. Vijay pulled a familiar bottle from his khaki knapsack. He said he needed a drink. I agreed. It was the first of many such agreements.

The years moved on. Vijay and Kavery got married. There were few people I admired more than Kavery, both for her dedication as a doctor and for her dedication to her writing. Not to mention her dedication to Vijay. In 2008, I invited them both to an international conference at the Institute of Advanced Study in Shimla. The conference was called 'Writing the Future'. Vijay and Kavery were a handsome couple; they made a proper impression on the assorted Australians, Englishmen, Indian academics. If anyone could write the future, they could. However, I noted that Vijay had turned more obstreperous than ever. He was, to borrow a description of him from Dom Moraes, 'a flamingo' among pusillanimous professorial ducks. And so, there may have been squabbles and whispers. Through it all, language remained Vijay's magnificent obsession; drink more than ever his constant companion. I felt we had grown apart, that I had been gentrified and domesticated by Delhi while Vijay had spent time away in Bihar, writing about another country, a vital set of truths.

Vijay was that rare individual, a man ever in search of inconvenient truths who was not averse to compelling his interlocutors to face up to such truths as well. I remember I once tried to thank Vijay for dedicating his book *Language as an Ethic* to me. Foolishly ready as I was to be flattered, Vijay would have none of my namby pamby, gendered twittering: 'I only did that,' he said to me, grinning dismissively, 'because I did not want you to destroy the book.' I'm still trying to figure out what Vijay meant. Kill *Language* in a review? Talk it down? Give it the evil eye? I think he was perhaps indicating that his was no act of base praise. He was defending his commitment to the language ethic from academic marauders like me who might attack simply because their own limited ethic consisted in nothing better than mere arid skepticism, a sort of thoughtless slash and burn. Was that what he meant? When I do work out Vijay's complex meaning, I promise him another poem.

Meanwhile, the enigmatic terseness of Vijay's dedication continues to be instructive: *For Rukmini Bhaya Nair*, followed by a line from one of my poems which was really a reprise of Noam Chomsky's famous line concerning semantic contradictions in language, which he in turn had borrowed from yet another obscure poet: *Colourless green ideas sleep furiously*. A quote by Vijay of a poem of mine which was a quote of Chomsky's quote from a third poet. A braid of quotations. What did it signify?

There was only one word in that Chomsky quote that really captured Vijay's sense of *elan vital* or what Henri Bergson called 'creative evolution'. That word was 'ideas'. His output was not prodigious: two volume of poems, *Gemini I*, shared with Jeet Thayil (1992), and *First Infinities* (2015) twenty-three years later; two books of non-fiction, *Bihar Is in the Eye of the Beholder* (2000) and *Language as an Ethic* (2003); and a single work of translation *Puntanam and Melpattur: Two Measures of Bhakti* (2009)—but it was enough to pencil him into posterity. This is surely because Vijay was incapable of being colourless, *ever*. Nor was he ever 'green with envy' for the bounteous gifts others received, not in the least. He may have been furious occasionally, but fury was not really in his nature; nor a sleepy acceptance of the quotidian world.

The truth is that for Vijay, there could be no ideas, no communion of minds, no truths without language, *simpliciter*.

That was his ethic in all his books; today, that stubborn allegiance has placed him in the company of immortals.

Like the railway lines in 'Madras Central', elegiac lines from Wilde (*For each man kills the thing he loves / Yet each man does not die*) and Milton (*For Lycidas is dead*), from Donne (*Death, be not proud*) and Shakespeare (*What's he to Hecuba or Hecuba to him that he should weep for her?*) now crisscross in my head. They are poetic tributes from the great masters of the English language to Vijay, I recognize—but his own fine lines definitively override theirs.

> The long rails recline into a distance
> Where tomorrow will come before I know it.
> I cannot be in two places at once:
> That is axiomatic....
>
> Terrifying
> To think we have such power to alter our states,
> Order comings and goings: know where we are not wanted
> And carry our unwantedness somewhere else.

Well, as usual, Vijay has managed to transcend his own axiom. Today, he is indeed in two places at once, he is 'most wanted' and the power of his language to alter our states will remain potent for a long while to come. Also, my imperfect, stalled, peahen poem is done.

Hecuba and Him
(For Vijay Nambisan)

> what's Hecuba to him?
> or he to Hecuba

that she should
weep for him?

all morning
on the feathered grass
the old peahen and I—
mourning

all dowdy brown
and scruffy green
this peahen's just a joke
like me—but for her crown

all uppity regal
and rhinestone gleam—
as if she's no old peahen
but peacock and eagle

all rolled into one—
on the feathered grass
this old peahen and I
together and alone

weep for him as squawky loud
as we would for Hecuba
where, o where has he gone
this breaking dawn?

Now, a year after his death, rereading his poetry, I realize that Vijay is likely to have had a pretty good idea of where he was going. In my grounded estate, in standard IIT housing, I may have been trying desperately to summon up peahens, eagles and whatnot in an effort to reach out to a friend I could not quite believe had died. Still and all, I did not then understand that Vijay's favourite poetic bird was, in fact, not the swan but the duck. For him the humble duck, its webbed feet wobbling, was a metonym for the unsteady balance of life and death, of the meeting of air, water and earth. In the coda to this introduction, I begin with an unusual word that Vijay uses as the title of one of his last poems and end with the problem of the ducks:

Integument

These 'Collected Poems' of Vijay's have an obvious tripartite structure, beginning with the early poems in *Gemini I*, going on to the substantial middle collection *First Infinities* and ending with a last clutch of unpublished *New Poems*. Released when Vijay was barely 30, *Gemini I*, as is to be expected, is the work of a young man whose umbilical cord is not quite cut yet. Family portraits dominate this volume.

First Infinities, on the other hand, has itself a sophisticated triadic structure. The title refers to the mathematical 'Aleph' series of countable cardinal numbers and the volume is further cleverly fashioned in terms of three words you might actually encounter in an accountant's ledger—namely, 'Loss', 'Balance' and 'Profit'. Thus, the abstract world of numbers merges with the mundane world of everyday business in a wonderful sleight of hand. In this volume, the poems are about going in and out of hospital, of regaining a delicate mental balance through a deep rereading of myth and folktale, and about emerging from one's ordeals with perhaps a small margin of profit, of optimism and hope.

What, though, do we make of the *New Poems*, published here for the first time? I believe we could read these poems as continuing commentaries on the loss and profit balance sheets of life that were a principal metaphor in *First Infinities*. We could also read into them an exciting theoretical extension of the Aleph set. The cardinal numbers are the 'first infinities', usually contrasted with a set of terms associated with 'infinity' rather than cardinality. Had Vijay lived, I believe he might have pursued this challenging mathematical distinction in his poetry. Indeed, I think he did make a cautious move in this direction in some of his new poetry, exploring regions of experience that go beyond countable cardinality. In this poetry, Vijay tests the limits of bodily sensation and its parameters, questions 'the evidence of my senses'. Consider, for instance, the intriguing notion of 'integument' that he introduces in a poem of that name. A gloss on this unusual word may be in order here: an 'integument' is a protective outer covering, in animals and plants, such as the skin or hide. Vijay writes:

> Hold me tight, my skin, I fear you may burst
> Before your time with ripeness, and show the world
> My red heart of anger. Hold me tight, I pray,
> That I may not be compelled to face the worst
> With worser still. What, will this blood be shed
> From mere longing, saying what cannot be said?
>
> Yet burst if you will, for I well know
> Inside, that inside is another wall

> Which will hold off anything that may call
> For your destruction. That shield's blazons show
> Like a mirror, the vitals of compassion.
> It can never burst in such a fashion.
> A second skin is something more than skin.

We depend on these 'skins' to distinguish objects form one another, to count populations of human beings, cattle, trees—and ducks. Were integuments, the 'walls within walls', to burst, we would be prone to destruction. Countability and accountability would both be lost, boundaries dissolved, infinities entertained. For Vijay, ducks, unlike terrestrial peacocks and aerial eagles, seemed to inhabit this border between the infinities of water bodies and earth bodies. In *First Infinities*, he has already observed this changeling nature of ducks. They belie the evidence of the senses; they could be frogs or birds or crickets or even sound like a river but they are, in the end, 'only ducks'.

> When the rain stopped the ducks began their noise,
> Hoarse-throated, full-chested, and we heard them
> Away in the big house, after dinner, and my niece
> Asked, 'Are they bullfrogs?' I said yes, or perhaps birds.
> But I knew all the time they were only ducks.
>
> Their noise is incessant, like frogs or crickets.
> And sometimes to me it is like the river

A sustained series of duck vignettes in the new poems takes the ambiguity of the metaphor much further. In 'Mach Duck' Vijay revisits the 'Mach number' in fluid dynamics, named after the physicist Ernst Mach, once again apparently corroborating my feeling that he is thinking in terms of extending number theory to poetry, playing gleefully with certain foundational concepts in science. In another duck poem, 'Original Sin', Vijay learns from ducks no less than the notion of self-sufficiency ('Ducks have, in water, all they really / Need, food and drink and exercise / And a tight refuge') while 'L'après-midi d'un Canard' discusses the social hierarchy of 'duck-hood':

> Ducks have, in water, a visible class
> And grace they completely lack on land.

'Double Bill' attributes to ducks the professional capacity to lead 'a kind of double life'.

> A duck
> Maybe thinks she has reason to hide
> What she does with her feet. She must float
> For no one must know she can walk on water.

After all this, it is hard to believe that ducks are not in fact Vijay's symbol for human nature, for our capacity to tread water, yet somehow stay afloat; keep secrets and yet show ourselves fully. It is a point Vijay makes in an ultimate duck poem, 'Buoyancy'. Ducks symbolize this sensation but it is not altogether a positive one.

> Ducks have, in water, a feeling that they are
> Not quite all there. That's why they keep looking down
> To see if their nether parts are still of the same
> Feather, that they're still together.
>   I too, sometimes
> Catch myself looking down to see if my feet

Are still on earth.
And so when I look up
I return where I belong, after long separation.

To return where one belongs, after long separation. What phrase could better capture our universal longing for home, for union and for liberation? In the title poem of this volume, 'These Were My Homes', Vijay tracks a path from the safe womb to the single 'bed in which to breathe my last of air'. I can think of few poets who have better traversed that eternal arc.

Rukmini Bhaya Nair
July 2018

GEMINI I

The Miracle of the Pomegranate

In the August rain the flowers are changing
The shape of the tree. It was light and airy,
Holding its colours high above the earth, arranging
For itself a crown with sure fingers. Now rudely laden
With miracles, it regards the wetness below.

Fruits swell in crimson and yellow, strange
To pluck from grey air. Is there nothing else to do
But life must poke its secrets up through the shoots,
Up past the leaves and into the flowers,
Filling them slowly as if trying on gloves;

Nothing to do but after the merest shower
It should be thrusting earth aside with green plumes
Simply to put the tree in proper perspective—
Unwanted things coming again and again to birth,
Ignoring the fact that the gardener's due tomorrow.

He'll mutter to himself, Nothing useless nothing wasted,
But the tree's grown so tall that half its prizes
Will only come to the wasteful bats and thieving
Squirrels, then be left to lose their colours, rotting,
Laying the secret bare to be sympathized with.

Reflections on May Day

Counting coins is no pursuit for a brave man.
Rather he should count the heads of his enemies
With a meataxe.
   So I tell the shopkeeper,
And the shopkeeper tells the wholesaler,
And the wholesaler relays the observation
To the producer, i.e. the farmer.
      Away
In Afghanistan, which is after all not
So very far off, that's where you should be,
The farmer replies to the wholesaler,
And the wholesaler conveys same to the
Shopkeeper, and so the shopkeeper tells me,
Leaning lightly on the scales.
     A proving ground
For other people's weapons is no battlefield,
I reply. I wonder where my enemies are.

Madras Central

The black train pulls in at the platform,
Hissing into silence like hot steel in water.
Tell the porters not to be so precipitate—
It is good, after a desperate journey,
To rest a moment with your perils upon you.

The long rails recline into a distance
Where tomorrow will come before I know it.
I cannot be in two places at once:
That is axiomatic. Come, we will go and drink
A filthy cup of tea in a filthy restaurant.

It is difficult to relax. But my head spins
Slower and slower as the journey recedes.
I do not think I shall smoke a cigarette now.
Time enough for that. Let me make sure first
For the hundredth time, that everything's complete.

My wallet's in my pocket; the white nylon bag
With the papers safe in its lining—fine;
The book and my notes are in the outside pocket;
The brown case is here with all its straps secure.
I have everything I began the journey with,

And also a memory of my setting out
When I was confused, so confused. Terrifying
To think we have such power to alter our states,
Order comings and goings: know where we're not wanted
And carry our unwantedness somewhere else.

paranoia/paranoia
For Krishna

You ran from the city so you could be alone.
There was something that knew you.

     You also knew
That it would follow you here, also,
To the wilderness;

     You ran not to be safe, but
Alone and facing it in isolation,
You might recognize it for what it was—
There was nothing here to conceal it, either.

You ran from the city to find a solitude
But now, suddenly, you are insecure—

You ran not to be safe, but, suddenly,
Safety has followed you from the city
And you do not know where else you can go.

Cats Have No Language

Cats have no language to tell their world.
The moon is a midsummer madness
That satisfies foolish chroniclers;
But their paws gloat on the captured mouse
—The slither beneath the stair—the silent bat
That drifted on a moonbeam into the house
Gashed a slitted eye into a flicker
And was gone. The moon is too much for the cat.

The light is too much for cats: that is why
At the human snarl behind the torch
The keen eyes turn slate, and a careless slouch
Replaces the studied artistry, frozen flash
Before the kill. They do not like the light
But have no language save the curving slash
And the sideways sculpture at a whisker's touch
Cats are dumb when they walk in the night.

Cats are clever at night, but the sun
Melts the moon's glitter out of their eyes,
Leaves them children's toys and the green trees.
Now how can fingers soothe the shoulder-knots,
Trust the silken purr, the kind eyes? Cat,
I know, I have seen her sleeping thoughts
Tense and stalk savagely in the night's peace.
But cats need no language to do all that.

The Attic

There is too much rubbish in the attic,
Unni, would you go up and see
What's worth keeping?

Grandmother, the temple doves are nesting there
And the floor is sifted with soft down.
The sills are occupied with their lovemaking,
And their throaty burbles fill the room with sound.

Unni, the doves have nested there for centuries,
But would you see what the attic holds?

Grandmother, bats hang from the rafters
And the corners reek of their peculiar smell.
One flew past my head suddenly,
Swerving away as if he didn't like it.
Grandmother, what makes them fly like that?

She sighs. Unni, the bats have flown there
Since I was a child, and for all I know
They are the same bats still. They always fly like that.
But what valuables are there in the attic?

Unni leaves hesitantly, and it is a long time
Before his footsteps sound the stairs again.
She waits, relieved.

     Grandmother, I am sorry,
But I found this piece of carved wood in the corner
By the teak chest, and was looking at it all this time.
Isn't it very pretty? Who made it?
Can I keep it?

  She is silent for a long while,
Her fingers groping for the secrets in the grain,
Her mind for words and faces. And then she says,
You may go out and play now, dear Unni.
I see there's much that is valuable in the attic.

She waits to hear his delighted shouts
In the courtyard by the well, then with slow
Time-burdened steps, feeling within herself
Every moment she has lived, acknowledging tiredly
Every wrinkle in her breasts, she begins to climb.

Diary of the Expedition

I

Every time we came to a difficult climb
The porters stopped dead, and indicated
With stubborn disobedience or much tiresome
Whining, that they could not proceed, weighted
As they were. We felt sorry for them, set
To a task whose glory they could not know
Or be ennobled by; but we had to go on, and
With great reluctance we would slaughter
One or two, to set an example to the rest.

II

Today we paused upon a lofty pinnacle,
The snows falling away among ravines and
Smooth slides, so curved and textured,
Like to a woman's hair. We could breathe
But with difficulty; and yet seeing, far off,
A bluer sky and a faint radiance lighting
The white expanses, we felt strangely cheered
And fancied ourselves closer to the gods.

I thought of home, and wondered again
At what nobility is in the human breast.

III

Our chief guide, a native, but one who's been
More disposed to serve (the rest are surly fellows)
Slipped today on a perilous path: without a cry
He was swallowed by the abyss. It is
A great blow, for we now have none with us
Who knows the journey well; but we must
Proceed; we cannot turn back, such dangers
Faced and overcome. We are much slower
Now, for often we cannot find the path. I put
My faith in God. These natives can't be trusted.

IV

The path gets worse and worse. It led us
Suddenly to the base of a great cliff, and
With much difficulty we led the horses up
Whinnying and nervous, with a massive wall
On one side and on the other a chasm
Like a gaping mouth. I forced myself
Not to look. But once we had reached the pass
I fancied it well worth the peril, for there
From the mountain's shoulder we saw the world lie open.

It was not until then that we realized
This is quite the highest peak in all these alps.
I raised the flag there, in the Emperor's name
And we laughed like boys and frolicked in the snow.
We go on more bravely; but our danger is great.

V

The horses have been abandoned. Several
Of our company weakened and were left
Behind. Today we came again to a mighty rock
And the path snaked about it like a winding
Thread. We did not have the spirit to attempt
Such an ascent. We have begun to skirt the rock,
But it will cost us several days. We have dwindled
To a handful of brave hearts, and our courage
Is pitifully husbanded against these alien snows.
It costs much pain to walk. The Lord have mercy.

VI

The last native guide (the rest I shot myself
When they refused to proceed) told me this hour
That we have reached the valley of our seeking.
I see no signs of Gold, but it must be indeed
A place of human habitation, for far below
The snows, there are orchards and what may be
Houses. I do not know how we will climb down.
I have no strength. I can no longer count

The members of my company, for always among them
I see the faces of those we have lost,
Brave and cheerful as they were at the start
Of this expedition, which has brought us to such
Despair, and to no treasures that can now gladden my
    heart.

Grandfather's Beard

                They call it grandfather's beard,
This windblown seed with white filaments:
I never saw such a beard on my grandfather,
But this feathery manifestation of air,
This oak heart holding the world to itself
And sending the winds to be so diffused,
It has something of the look in my grandfather's eye—
There were people, he said, unaffected by him
And there were those by whom he was not affected—
So also this secret (that I cannot associate
With any green plant clutching earth with its roots,
But seems to me rather the tangible form of a kiss,
Such a kiss as I would want to touch with my lips)
Floats on the light wind, and if you see it
It is there, and if you don't happen to
You are just as well off.
                I would like my poem to be
Like my grandfather's beard, to be airy
In the lean wind, to look up at the clouds
And laugh. There are people unaffected
By poetry, and there are those whom poetry
Disregards—I would like to write a poem
Like grandfather's beard.

Death of a Terrorist

The streets are hungry for the night,
From the sky they claw the red sun down,
Dying dripping on shopfronts and stones, avoiding
People's faces. The stains will fade. We walk
Hands in pockets, defining a silent road
Through black and grey crowds that give us room.

Moving west and moving a frontier with us,
Telltale hands in pockets because we are spies
And the Moon and Saturn are complex on our palms.
The long stares touch us, feel our shoulders, slip
To our feet, hushed upon the fall. Looking
Not to left or right, we find spaces in the throng.

The next streetlamp glows bright and hard. The day
Is given up. They gather round the fallen
Faultless in the dark. They draw apart for us.
'Is this the body?' 'It is.' Looking down,
We bring out our hands slowly, no suddenness,
And move our pocket handkerchiefs across dry lips.

The process is rehearsed, deliberate. We return,
Conscious of the things that love us. Think of nothing else
—But in a land that hates us so, shall we starve
Our feelings? Our eyes look not to left or right.
On the hills to the east the sun's last glitter
Fades

Ill Met by Moonlight

Crossing the floor with a woman in dance
I detest, my right thigh began to throb:
It was too much, the concatenation
Of omens—I stopped suddenly, and sprained
My ankle.
                Leading me tenderly off,
She asked was there anything she could do?
I kissed her cheek for answer
                              Curse the chance
Which caused it my left ankle that was sprained:
Had it been the right, I should have surely
Kissed her on the mouth. My tongue tingles still.

The balcony was bright with unopened flowers,
Unshed moonlight, unsaid words, unmanned me.
She sat by me and gently eased my foot.
This time I nuzzled her neck.
                          The gods above
Know that had only one moonbeam shone
Through the heavy night, I would have kissed her then.

Later still, we found ourselves in bed, and
Kept awake by pain, I said familiar spells,

Invoking myths and figures of shadow
To keep her by me.
                    What power can fail
That has so successfully, all these years,
Kept my left thigh from my right thigh's knowledge?

I write this guardedly, by pure moonlight.
She stirs, she says something sad of tone,
She kisses her pillow. I watch with care.
When my time comes to be possessed, I know
I shall play my part well, after long study.

The Garden Variety Show

See the black and white pups scamper on the grass.
The young buggers are having a good time.
They're her last litter. There she lies,
The old bitch, in the shade; her lean flank
Heaving with the strain of staying alive.

The pups know she's their mother, but they'll be
Forgetting it soon. They can get by without her,
Although just now it's easier to pretend
She's indispensable. She doesn't fake, however,
She knows it's past time for all that.

She lets them dig at her worn teats, looking off
Across the sun-green lawn and through the latticed wall,
With hardly the strength to lift her eyes higher.
Perhaps she can see the sky, too; on the horizon
Of her eye, there's surely a glimpse of blue.

She's always been a sensible bitch, always known
What was expected of her. These pups of hers,
They're big and healthy, but seem a little foolish.
Of course, you can't tell at their age. Maybe
They know, too, what is expected of pups.

That's a lizard by the gate. The pups see him
And jump for him, yelling and laughing. He's off,
Dislodging a few scraps of rust, flashing into
Some crevice by the wall. The pups saunter back
To their mother, but she'll have none of them.

With a yawn she turns over and shuts her eyes.
They look at her, then with philosophical shrugs
Stroll across to beg from me.

      Family relationships
Are not as complicated as they're made out to be,
I write in my notebook. It's doing as you would be done
  by
That saps the strength. I do what is expected of me.

Poetic Licence

When my grandfather grew to be an old man,
he was a little mad:
        his hair turned black again
and his voice held its own, and his eyes
asked incessantly for answer, an answer.

My mother would frown, and shake her head, and laugh;
but she would hold him, would roll his paan
and wipe his mouth.
               And later,
sitting by herself in the dusk,
she would be sad awhile.

For my grandfather was once a poet
        and some of the world's weight
had lain upon his shoulders.

Auto Da Fé

A brolga, I learned today, is an Australian bird
Like a crane, who performs an elaborate dance
To convince his beloved he is the fellow for her.
She seems to be persuaded, watching the tall fool strut
And smirk and flap his wings and dip his bill.
—How many thousands of years,
                      wonders the rapt ornithologist
Crouching in the weeds with the lakewater
                      lapping at his arse,
How many million acts of love
                      brought the ritual to this climax,
Simple and intricate as a Russian watch—
                      does the bird know,
Does it feel, does it have a sense of history? Can he evolve
The pattern from its roots, tell the dancer from the dance?

Notebook and pencil fall from his twitching fingers,
His mouth opens and closes, long threads of saliva
Stain his chin. Waving his arms in sincere imitation,
Bowing, preening, dancing forward
                      and back with little hops,
He tries to join in. Long-recessive genes
                      are pressed into service
But, his mechanisms in revolt, he can no longer fear

The stately neck of his rival now bearing him down,
The starved claws tearing at his loins,
           or see the redrimmed eyes,
The bill gouging out his face. In his lady's look,
As the ritual is completed, there is a hooded sympathy.

After Six Drinks

I am grieving for everything which has occurred
To put me where I am, and us where we are—
I am sorrowing even for what holds us—in a word,
For everything I am grieving without bar.

I am grieving for my friends who are laughing now,
Let them. My heart is filling so much it cannot speak.
Now they are laughing, see only tomorrow how
They will cry to God. But of course the gods are Greek

And they find it so funny, our small disaster.
...Someone was whispering that hearts are meant to
    break—
I am willing my heart to beat faster and faster,
Finishing life quickly. This is no ordinary ache.

I am pouring my sorrow into a little cup,
Just to drown the gods in—a libation, nothing more,
And when we are being happy and the roof is on the floor
Someone can reach out and casually drink me up.

Drums at Night

Drums at night remind me of a funeral
Where the rich flames lent their evanescence to
The living flesh gathered around, concentrated
Upon that gift to the darkness, consumed
With such easy irony by the light.

No one spoke of it, but making glorious
Their shame, they denied the possessive black
Behind; denied perhaps that the stars
Burned with no other fire. When the wood crackled
With sounds like words, it did not call their names.

But when the flimsy cage around the brain
Exploded, yielding at last intelligence
To the enemy, eyes were raised appalled,
Accusing; only the mechanical drums
Confirmed them in their need for ritual.

Holy, Holy

The rain threatens this ordinary day
With magic. Things that grow manifest,
Plainly, the unnatural: more sure
And permanent is the unwalked way,
Lifeless air, stone unencumbered
With feelings; not obsessed, therefore pure.

Yet even metal has a life that cries
For use, even crystals ask to be touched—
How much weaker are these green and clinging loves,
These hollow souls that populate the skies
With what they aspire to. Reality
In itself is content, and needs no proofs.

When I was young enough to treat these things
Without consciousness, I could cast my mind
Into that emptiness whereof all is made
And ask, without my imaginings,
What is?
     Nothing answered nothing, and in that space
I knew myself unliving, unafraid.

Flotsam

Waiting behind a wall
To see his actions in other men's eyes,
His thoughts became hopelessly horizontal:

He found his past, presents
Of time loosely packaged; losing himself,
He became assorted moments.

Wandering the streets
Of an ancient city, he saw people
By whose opinions he had lived; as a drunkard meets

Himself in the mirror,
He groped for familiar features, words
And eyes, and flesh; but they told him, easily,
How he was just something that had once occurred
In their dreams, an old-fashioned terror.

Biography

I live with the sound of the sea constantly in my ears,
    sniffing the tang of the salt wind.
I live among books and oppressed peoples, in pyramids
    and in groves of sandalwood and alabaster.
I live with the shrinking blue sky above and beyond me,
    with a pale planet in my dreams.
I live with a man who is what I am but bears no name.

Born without a language and in the frightened
    iconoclasm of my age,
I have tasted words, chewed words, eaten words,
I have fashioned out of words feelings multifarious
    in colour and texture,
I have burdened words with a soul whose sins are my own.

I lived among the vast riches of my people,
    but could not spend my wealth.
I let the men my grandmother told me of become the gods
    of an unsophisticated tribe.
I touched the sky and sea with an empty iron hand
And let a soft silken one roam subtly through my hair.

Base Indian, who waited a generation to find
    you are all his fathers left him,
Who shall wait on you at table, who shall slay for you,
    who shall supplicate, who weep?

Narcissus in the Drought

Watch thirstily the dry hollows etched sharp in the sun,
The tortured lives reconciled to death, until
The craving will suffice, and remembered waters fill
The long naked channels, gurgling run
Or shimmer like mirages in exhausted eyes.

Wait, wait in the heat, stale air and aching heat,
Wait among the stifled shapes and attempt to keep
In vanished rivers drowned, or beneath the earth and deep,
A memory of peace; beneath six feet
Of dying rock, in a cool, dank hollow underground.

Here there is no relief—this changelessness is worst—
But one thin ghost of shadow at which I ever stare:
Dry and faint as dust, it seems with me to share
A need for more than water, a thirst
That water cannot assuage, but water must.

I will the flickering image to move towards the shore:
There is no stream; but my memory will flow
Always along its course. Though remembrance is slow
And not enough, yet ever more and more
The stream sounds in my ears,
                    with a voice both clear and hoarse.
There is flood in the air; in the mouth, great thirst,

A prayer to the shadow to move a little more
Towards a vision I know possessed me there before.
I cannot hope to live now; but first
It must hurt somewhat, to perish, not knowing why.

FIRST INFINITIES

Loss

Dirge

The poets die like flies but I am lying slightly to one side,
Contented in my Spain or Siam, content too to keep my
   hide.
How well they wrote, those friends now fettered, how the
   Indo-Anglian tongue
Allowed them to be lovely-lettered, their lives lived when
   the world was young.
I'll live and hold my words in, for I am wearied of
   hypothesis;
And, in place of getting glory, kisses take from my missis.

Then the world shone, by their showing; then publishers
   seemed to care;
Then calls for cheques of last year's owing did not fall on
   empty air.
Then newspapers asked them for pieces; and printed them
   unchanged; and paid;
But now there are so many wheezes which make the craft a
   thrifty trade.
In a wilder whirl of weeklies, tabloids titting on page
   threes,

I will shirk my duty meekly and kisses take from my missis.

They did not care much what the world said: they taught
    it instead how to speak.
They did not, when a poem pleaded, to meetings go in
    Mozambique.
But I will stay my poems, spending strength now with a
    shriller pen
My theme and language both defending, to live fourscore
    years and ten.
And if it prove my prime is over, if I've no chance at
    wordly bliss
Why I will spurn so false a lover and kisses take from my
    missis.

This hand once penned those poems: never shall I find so
    true a friend.
I've a thirst for all forever, but the lines come to an end.
So Arun and Dom and Nissim—I will shun their hard-
    earned grief
And much though I will always miss 'em, in softer
    shadows find relief.
And when I'm ninety and young writers ask why I wrote
    no more than this
I will answer, 'But, you blighters! I kisses took from my
    missis.'

Words from the Dying City Came
For Sagari

Words from the dying city came
As a thirsty man asks for water
And the bougainvillaea climbed the walls of the white
    house
Far from the slaughter.

A man sits high by a luminous window
Where the white doves ruffle their restless feathers.
And he hears the dying city as clearly as he hears
The bees in the bougainvillaea in the fine March weather.

The man by the window remembers last summer
In the doomed city. He sees the jacaranda flame against
    the sky.
And he knows it is useless, in another time and place
To listen to a city that must die.

Ducks

They hammered in the stakes and wound the long nets
    round,
Blue nets of nylon, about as high as where
They wound their dhotis, and I wondered as
I sat by the raining window what the blue meant,
The blue circles in the wet square of pasture.

Then at evening the boys drove up the ducks
From the river, squat and uncomplaining,
They herded them here and prisoned them in the
Blue cages. Then they went away. The rain
Sobbed till nightfall in the tamarind trees.

When the rain stopped the ducks began their noise,
Hoarse-throated, full-chested, and we heard them
Away in the big house, after dinner, and my niece
Asked, 'Are they bullfrogs?' I said yes, or perhaps birds.
But I knew all the time they were only ducks.

Their noise is incessant, like frogs or crickets.
And sometimes to me it is like the river
A mile or two away, groaning at its strength.
Or like the rain as it winds the teak groves through.
Or sometimes, to me, like the song of birds.

I am still wondering what they're doing there,
What's being done to them. As I write
Again the rain is washing the still morning small
And the ducks are silent, not at all thinking
What manner of beast creates these hours of sleep.

The Hole in the Earth

There is a hole through to the earth's bowels,
I glimpsed it yesterday, outside the gate,
A view of voided ground yielding voiceless vowels,
Saying without speaking; and through what ways
Winding, through what beatitude, what hate,
What hope of sanctity I do not know
It goes because last night I knew my place
Was not to know. Then waking in my sleep
I felt by day my fate and I could go
Down unwalkable roads beyond all name
Of nothingness, discover what they keep
Below of us without knowledge of day.
So I prepared; but today the workmen came,
Replaced the manhole cover, and went away.

Kalki

Difficult, now, to predicate order.
The wheel spins without weight at a careless touch.
Those who stand alone are always reclaimed
And the mobs conjugate at every border.
Who remains to guide me, how or how much
Shall I give of my gifts. Coming proclaimed
In other ages I brought a great prize
To my seekers in unconfounded peace.
Elsewhere I returned fire with fire, ice with ice

And bore a sword to those who would not fight.
Now I am ignored in hourly agonies.
My foolish news of the conclusive war
Comes to the inconsequential dead. My might
Is lonely: An unpeopled avatar.

Millennium

There was not much light in the world when we left.
The stairs were dank and smelled of anger.
At their foot was a heap of straw, soaked in blood:
We did not ask whose, for all was conjecture, and this
Fresh sign would have yielded us little more.

They say there are signs in all things; well, there were
Some we could have done without that day. For the sun set
The instant we had emerged from the passage-way
And we had to grope our road to the little shed where,
Little and unannounced, our mission lay.

Frost steamed the air. Our blood pulsed thin and shrill.
My brother pushed open the door. In the wild light
Of a torch, we saw the mother's breast was white and
    plump,
And the child's lips were red as any rose. None of us
Dared hesitate, or be afraid; we drew our swords.

It is long after that I tell this, and it may differ
From the tales you must have heard. What matters?
There was no light in the world when we did our deed.
There is no light now. Is it at all possible
That I should say more or less than that I know?

Yes. I have heard the stories. Yes, there was some talk
Of a brave man whose bravery passed all foolishness.
Yes, we are a weak people now but we were not so
When lured by gold but hardly less by strength
We let our faith die and put away our books
And enrolled ourselves under the Idumean.

He was a false king, at last, but what would you have?
There have been falser. One rules now, in Rome.
But this one thing I can say, because upon my steel
There sang the blood, and almost on my lips: with
That sword which now rotten hangs upon the wall,
With that blade and no other, I slew David's heir.

———

Diogenes

The watchman has lighted his lamp. Outside
The guarded houses, night is complete.

I hear his staff thud, thud. Hammering smooth,
Straightening the paths of many feet.

They are unselfconscious in the day. In the dark
They try to be silent, overcome

By knowledge that life is very far away.
It is in the attempt they become

Spies and strangers, betraying without will
Minds with a purpose, going somewhere.

The watchman follows. In open night
With impartial staff he shadows them,
Covering up motives that lay bare.

———

Elizabeth Oomanchery

Elizabeth Oomanchery
The celebrated poetess
Went to the corner shop
To buy a loaf of bread.
The shopman said, 'Excuse me,
'Aren't you Elizabeth Oomanchery,
'The celebrated poetess?'
So Elizabeth Oomanchery went home.

Elizabeth Oomanchery
Sat at her desk one evening
To write herself a poem.
The poem asked, 'Excuse me,

'Aren't you Elizabeth Oomanchery,
'The celebrated poetess?'
Elizabeth Oomanchery
Said 'Yes,'
So the poem went home.

———

Aswatthama

Whenever he put on his high-soled shoes
And came to town, we all felt out of place:
He was a man to whom nothing is news
Although he wore his boredom with fine grace
And his kindness was apparent in his face.

He'd talk with us of Love, or Art, the while
We sat on the sofa and sipped our drinks;
But his sudden pauses, his secret smile—
We would half-say, I wonder what he thinks.
Yet nothing he said would supply us the links.

Oh, he was charming, and could always be
Relied upon to make an evening go;
But suddenly he would look at you, and see
—Well, what? and you would feel leaden, and slow.
But we all liked him. At least, I suppose so.

And then he came no more. We do not talk
Of him, but sometimes, when the passing hours

Oppress, we fall silent, as if he should walk
In at the door. But the memory sours.
Even his silences were different from ours.

Snow

Crisp in the winter's morning,
Softly all through the night,
What is this without warning.
    Falling and white?

    I have never seen snow
    But I can imagine it quite—
    Not how it tastes, but I know
        It falls and is white.

        One morning I'll open the door
        To bring in the morning's milk,
        And all around there'll be snow—
            Fallen and still.

            How I'll roll in the stuff!
            How I'll tumble and spin!
            Until the neighbours cry, Enough!
                And send me back in.

Age Speaks to Age

My forefathers came here so many years ago,
Even the land may now have forgotten. —You ask
Whether the land loved them? I do not know,

But they were insistent upon their rights:
They said a people such as were settled here,
Without a tongue with which to read or write

Were not of God, but little better than
The beasts within the jungle, or the birds
Who cannot know what it is to be a Man.

What do you say, little one? That the birds
And beasts speak, too? Yes, when I was young
I could hear things that were said without words.

So said the people that my fathers' fathers found:
'We read our past and future in the skies
And write our present on this hallowed ground—

'What need of more?'—The runes that flowed and shone
Upon his bright blade, our chieftain showed them then.
What need of more? Our swords were steel; theirs, stone.

So with steel we wrote our story. There is silence
Now through the land—all but our talk, our songs,

The texts we write and all the noble deeds that men's

Arms find to do. In silence drop the tears
Of rain; silent the thunder speaks; silent
The seasons pass, and say no new things in our ears.

Christ Stopped Here
'Carlo Levi, celebrated author of Christ Stopped at Eboli...'
—Pablo Neruda, *Memoirs*

How white the snowdrifts in the pass!
how green the grass
down there in the plains;
The earth not showing,
the mountains yet growing,
                growing still...
And like memories of another year
the prints of long-dead palms
                upon the trees,
                the cruel trees
which lance into the sky... I am afraid
that someone else must live as I did,
                must die...

Here, where the grasses grow
                beneath the snow
or here, lie
                beneath the snow:

Christ stopped here.

    (song for two voices)
Jesu, fruit of God's believing
In glory and an end to grieving,
Embrace me as you only can,
Make into me a little man.

Jesu, in the rock or crystal
Conceptualized a little seed:
But from the amber came a pistol;
What grew then was only my need.

Here in the hills
    that may or may not stand at Eboli
crafted of a magic name
whose magic I may understand
and may not,
    here in the hills
are snow, and the green grass
    and a red sun:
But come, into the shade
    (I am afraid
    to relive what has passed)
and you will see upon the tree
(the tree is old and haughty, its bark
 is like many winters), upon the tree

the prints of many palms
as if groping through the dark:

Beside, in the snow
    or grass, I do not know
but it is trampled by feet
    (I have been here before!)
feet waiting for an hour,
Just one hour, and no more:

And look more closely, you will find
some blood
    ah, that is nothing, never mind;
Some crusts of bread, some crumbs of cheese
        (a little peace)
and some ash—oh, holy ash!—
from a cheap cigar.
      Yes, Christ stopped here.

    (as if from above)
He carved upon rock and on river and reed,
He carved upon snow all the soul of his need.
His hand never shook, his fingers aye pressed,
But his mind, ah! his mind—it was never at rest.

      Leaving the alien hills
that have seen me before,
felt my need again: to harvest
Something else, some new grain
unused by man...
    so I must down to the plain,
to live as someone else a while,
to work hard, to sweat, to smile,

to feel my palms blistered, not soft as before
                    (to smoke no more)

I am come out from under the tall trees
                    inauspicious of memory

So leave this place
                    but I am still afraid:
I have seen no ghost, no familiar face
that smiled at my trouble, nor said,
Friend, you have been here before, and it is all
Vanity, vanity to imagine you suffer
for you must live again, and live
          again
                    But I am afraid
For what if I go down to the plains
          and they are bare, if there is
no green grass to remind me of my need,
          no amber, and no seed—

But what if in the clouds there grows
a face—or in the water, clear water
a face—or in the wind, gently brushing
my face like cobwebs in moonlight

And it's a face that I have seen before
or if upon the young trees, whose bark
is like an infant's skin, I should see
                    the cruel palms

Should I not be possessed again by my fear?
My memories of another long-passed year?
Shall I have none, no one loved and dear
                    and no one to despise?

And stop and know
        a weight bears down upon my eyes
                know

Christ stopped here.

―――――

Chyavana

When the great sage immured his narrow law
Within the anthill, that his confined eye
Might open inward, and stare upon the truth,
His sacrifice was vain; for he little thought
That human innocence would interfere,
The silly girl would poke the thorn within,
Convert metaphor into fact, and show
What he deemed illusion was really so.

That was the test: to see if he would smile
And thank the princess, and say, 'Now this anthill
'Is quite unnecessary, and all my life
'I'm freed of temptation'; and so grow wise

And the three worlds would shake to see the Man.
But he, blind fool, only roared in rage
(Which quite tickled Fate) like an overgrown boy
Whose toy's broken, and wants another's to keep.

So satisfied, the primal fancy curled
Within the actions of the living world
Winked its broad eye, and went back to sleep.

The Deserted Temple
Sravanabelagola

The god is gone. His cave is bare.
    In shadow from the sun
The clotted bats hang from the roof.
    Below, the scorpions run
And pious folk no longer come
    Lest evil should be done.

Ruins of flowers on the floor
    Bear imprints of his feet.
They point through the door into
    The many-miraged heat.
His voice was heard. His fragrance kept
    This prisoned air once sweet.

His voice was heard: It told his tribe

> To leave this sun-cursed hill.
> They went, and left his dwelling here.
> > They went; it was his will.
> Who piled these stones knows when he comes
> > And where he stays until.

To HST

Why do they always couple 'law' with 'order'?
Who the hell are 'they', anyway?

Our progress must be with faltering steps:
Entropic; its fruit, fruitlessness.

Wave a hand and dissolve a window,
Stretch a smile into its component parts,

Each fragment a wholly pointless grin
Breaking the glue of polite conversation.

Rip up the paving-stones with tender hands,
Scatter the seeds of dragons; then retire

Peacefully into some private hell
Kept desolate by a troop of frustrated Boy Scouts.

Something Rich and Strange

He was past patience when he threw in his lot
With the sea. He abandoned himself to the sweep
And swell of water, putting away the thought
That this was permanent and could not be cured
By any charm of his. He would endure
What the neighbours said. Now there was only sleep.

His fingers rose and fell upon the tide,
Weightless as his mind, and his legs suddenly twitched
As if they would feel the earth. He did not care
For his body now—it too would be pitched
Loveless down, away from light. Now that his pride
Was committed, his flesh had little to bear.

He lifted himself to see it all again,
To seize the moment. It wasn't right. A lack
Of decision, even now—where was the pain,
Where the drama, the completeness? What had he missed?
He was sad at last. His head settled back,
Marring the ceramic. The soap fell from his fist.

Medical Entry

Arteriosclerosis: A condition of
The heart eventuated by too
Much vanity, too little love
For what we have caused to produce
Us; Insecurity of a few
Glands; Valiant attempts to choose
Between various failings, an
Effort to close in oneself the
Effortless secret of man.

Conditional upon the heart's own
Involuntary needs is
This condition, sometimes known
As 'Hardening': Hard Times, Hard Cheese
Are like phrases. Consequently this
Entangles the faculties
In perceiving it as a tonic
For jaded life; After all the
Fact remains that death is chronic.

Prognosis: Grave. Certain medicines
Have palliative effects which
Are salutary, reducing
Ante-mortem rigor mortis,
Ocular Jaundice (*vide* a Stitch
In Time) and pain. Accidental
Kindnesses are performed by the
Dying, but life remains fatal.

Mind the Gap

Mind the gap. The seasons spoil and change
But the gap is to be minded. Not mended, mind,
For each to each must forever be strange:
Mind the gap. There, that's a splendid chap.
    Please mind the gap.

We may look ahead or read *The Daily Mail*,
We may study the ads and even find
The perfect holiday; but on this tunnelled trail
We mind the gap. That's a splendid chap.
    Please mind the gap.

Stiffly we sit. Our empires are within
And must not touch each other. Behind,
In some holey station, musicians swing.
But we mind the gap. We are splendid chaps.
    Please mind the gap.

We travel each to a peculiar end,
Rock with the rock, grind with metallic grind
And will not recognize enemy nor friend.
Mind the gap. Yes, that's a splendid chap.
    Please mind the gap.

I mind my business and watch the seasons mend.

Nila in Flood Time

Nila is a local name for the Bharatapuzha, which flows across north-central Kerala to the Arabian Sea

Mornings in late July
Stern in the steel-grey skies
Warnings of thunder cried
    Reminders of gain

Looked at the hard earth which
Spoke of our dearth, and rich
Smoke curled over the bridge
    Praying for rain.

Nila lay cold and stark
Silver though was her spark
Filament of the dark
    Thread in the sun

River so kind and cool
Reliever of summer's rule
Giver when to our cruel
    Loom she be spun.

Who shall applaud her now?
When in thrall this is how
The call of the arrow
    Summons the bow:

In coil on coil the snake
Steels all her strength to make
Always without mistake
    That one springing blow.

    2

Slowly she rose above
Lowly reef, spit and cove
Flowed to that one remove
    Beneath the town

Then broke the waters pent
One stroke the pattern rent
Dark cloaked the firmament
    The rain came down.

Rising to embrace us
Twining through embrasures
Smiling she increases
    Giver of wealth—

Winding where she pleases
Minding no man-measures
Why should she displace us
    But for our health.

Swelling a mile each way
Felling the palms to lie
Telling their tales to grey
    Unmannered sky

Motionless in her sweep
Ocean is not more deep
Chosen secrets to keep
    Than this of eye.

3

Blood and bone cannot stand
Flood and famine at hand
Rudely we understand
    The day is now

One hour from the end
All ours may pretend
But powers of a friend
    Have become foe.

How she batters the wall!
How she gathers her all
Howling the southwest falls
    Upon a shore

That yesterday was ours
That festival and flowers
And arrested lovers
    Kept tame ever more.

Lashing our flesh with cane
Smashing to mud again
Cash and the hoarded grain
    And our tall walls

Believe, animals yet
Relive, or else forget
To scrive the alphabet
    At that one call.

        4

Goddess or madness, this
Glorious gladness is
Tore from us anxieties
    Living a lie

Storm and suddenness shook
Form from fate, eye from look
Dormant the master woke
    O thus to die.

Brown corpses rent across
Town, village counted loss
Blown and battered alas
    We are still here

River we worshipped once
Stealer of spoiled sons
Deceiver, while she runs
    What should we fear.

Fever of sacrifice:
Ever the victim vies
With the haruspices'
    Vision of time:

Grey water running free
Straight to tomorrow's sea
Faith that I cannot keep
    Go, and keep mine.

Balance

To the Lord of the Dance

To you the falling flower turns
And asks for rest: Your petalled foot
Poised lightly on the mortal breast,
Smile on me, Lord, until it burns
Me to be here where freedom is,
Waiting upon a little wind
Between this life and that your death.

Eternity, infinity
Are fruits come of a yielding tree
Which listens to the laughing wind,
Imagining that it is free.
My pain is still the pain of years
That whisper through the living air:
We will be, although you fall.

Destroyer, dance, and let me be
One with the earth your stamping shakes;
A flower is a promise, all
Ignorant of the weight it takes;
Let me be earth, let me prepare

The guilty stem and grasping root
And let all that would pass me, go.

Let freedom go: Nothing remains,
Nothing is true till shadow's end,
Nothing I see except the shape
Ecstatic in the dance begun
To which the falling flower turns,
Asking, Thus?
    while the wind maintains,
Alas my child, your dance is done.

———

Spider

There is a season known only to spiders
Which falls usually between June and September
(Though in some places it comes as early as April)
When they all have licence to crawl out of their own
Accredited crannies, and spin webs where they like.

This is a great offence to careful housewives
(Especially to those who are afraid of spiders)
—Suddenly to see a fat black bounty squatting
In a nook that was spotless an hour ago
Is enough to give anybody the hiccups.

There is a cure, however, as there is one
For all ills except those which breed in the heart

—Wait for the round white eggs of the gecko to hatch,
And carry off the hatchlings, as many as you need,
And secrete one in each violated corner,

And no spider will spin again there that season.
I was taught this by a truthful friend who has since
Transmuted himself. He was so devoted to spiders
That he decided to do the irrevocable,
Some time ago, and the last I heard from him was
                                                    Splatch!

Ilyushin

But it was real, she said, I know I saw a plane
Cut through the silver clouds with a more silver flame;
Why do you lie to me so? Why so leave a stain
On all that is between us?—I said, but hear me—

Oh, she said, you think that you will steer me
Out of my own opinions. Why do you fear me
When I tell truth? You saw, you were near me,
And I know what I saw—I said, but there is more—

You are so good at words, she said, you have in store
So many that make me look more stupid than before;
But that was no illusion, I saw it as it tore
Across the heavens—I said, let me explain—

De Maupussant's Lover

                The smell of you
Is sometimes in my nostrils, and the warm
Corruption of your breath upon my cheek,
And the remembered shape of you
Will sometimes turn and tighten in my arms
And fill my sleep.

                And tell of you
What I may, how faithless you have been,
How cruel, how true
Are ghosts that haunt my bed,
Your lips will only mock me with a smile
Or open in a death's-head grin;
And as I close them with a kiss, I seal
A letter from exile.

Lady with Parrot
For Gowri

                Parrot
            sweet parrot
        sweet parrot in a cage
              speak to me

and I will give you honeyed milk
      to keep sweet your tongue:

                    whisper one word to me.

                            Moon,
                        hornèd moon,
                    Lord of the hornèd moon,
                Lord of the city of the hornèd moon

                        by the refulgent sea:

                                parrot,
                            sweet parrot,
                        sweet parrot in a cage,

                        whisper His name to me.

                            ———

Bhima in the Forest

Of the flesh of the bull
And the flesh of the fowl
And the flesh of the blue deer
I have eaten.

        Of the blood
Of the hare, and the blood
Of the ram, and the blood
Of the peacock I have drunk.

Tell me, where is the snake
To spoil me, where is the tiger
To tear me, for I am brother
In my body, to all beasts.

When Suddenly the Poems Die

When suddenly the poems die
Away, when the pen lies bereft
Of striving hand, what use the day's
Long words, of pretence what is left?

It is like waking from a dream
Within a dream to find the night
Has just begun, and all that seemed
Substantial has still to be done.

So, love, the dull days without you
Are full of something new to come—
The poems that I will make true
Were born in this interregnum.

The Door

She shut the door because upon the other side
There was the voice of one for whom she once had cared:
    She shut the door.

'Open!' he cried, 'for there are things that I must say
'Which you must hear—which will mean much to both of
  us—
    'Open!' he cried.

Remembering how he had marched in thus before,
She turned away and stopped her ears to all his words.
    Remembering.

'When I asked you whether one day you'd shut me out,'
He said with bitterness, 'You replied with a kiss
    'When I asked you!'

She wondered why the words we say to those we want
Sometimes resound in worlds where we have never lived
    —She wondered why.

'You must have faith,' he said, 'although to you our love
'Appears to limp; with you I'm strong, you're strong with
  me
    '—You must have faith!'

She opened all her mind to all that she had lived,
She summoned all the strength she'd had and turned the key,
      She opened all.

He'd never been a man to whom her strength was new;
He'd never thought her precious all was hope enough;
      He'd never been.

The Nuns

The nuns are small and white and starch,
The nuns are tall and white and march
Stiffly in their virgin shrouds.
I do not know where they are from,
Where they will go and why they come,
But they always seem to know:
Eyes downcast and backbone straight,
Stockinged feet and swaddled gait,
I wonder where they think they go.

O ladies who have seen the light!
Sisters! I, a sybarite,
Would like to know where you are from,
Where you will go and why you come,
But your purpose frightens me.
I'm afraid you will make reply:
We go to heaven; so will you

If you have faith—what can I do
Who only know that I must die?

I will not ask. But sisters dear,
Whose purpose seems thus one and clear,
I—I'm only a little guy
Who only knows that he must die;
I know my passions can't match yours,
For I weep at failing, yet
Find comfort in a cigarette—
But—do you have no time to rest?
Must you strive so to be blest?

Once, within the Lord's chapel
I saw amidst the pealing bells
A stone maiden with dreaming eyes,
Her arms so raised that as she blessed
She held what vastness to her breast
And stood there—
        Sisters, if you will,
Stop! Dream that heaven where you'll rise,
Hold it in your inmost eyes
And stand a moment stony still.

To Have Been Written in Urdu

All the world, it seems, knows I like to drink:
How few know how well I like to be sober.

I like to touch darkness, sometimes, with steady fingers,
Not bound it round with mists and bright fuzzy lights.

I like to hear my thoughts as they drop one by one
On to a page, into a well, in a black brimless sea.
I do not always like to have to thresh around
To find the particular one that should feed at my breast.

I like sometimes to know that this is how to go,
Not reach a place for lack of other places to have gone.

I need, sometimes, to form a face which is a face,
Not a landscape of eyes and nose and mouth and eyeless
    gaze.

I like to look into the distance and see distances
And know that I will never know them as a familiar place:
Not find myself, when I want to be alone,
Surrounded by familiar places that have come from afar.

So many people seem to know that I like to drink
Whom I should never dream of informing that I was
    sober—

So why should I lie to them, as sober men do,
And insist they inhabit the world in which I live?

Śankuntala

Under the blue mountain, in the flowering cloud's shade
Where the earth is soft to the press of a maiden's foot
By a little river which laughs as it were wine
Upon a grassy breast of earth that the first gods made
Listening to the leaves fashion the wind's flute
She stares across the glade and wonders what she'll find.

Carelessly tearing the jasmine that clings to her black hair
Letting the fragrant fragments float upon the stream
Or giving them to the wind in payment for his tune
Half-hearing whispered secrets which the tall jungle lords
    share
Sensing that all is magic, prelude to birth, a dream
She looks beyond the far hills and knows it will be soon.

The forest deer devour her with their large longing eyes.
A shape with black and tawny stripes stops a moment his
    pursuit.
Within the stream the gleaming fishes quiver once,
    silently.
The earth breathes deep and shivers in long delicious
    surprise.
All life is still, all life is here within her life, but mute
In that one breath she senses death and anticipates me.

———

Mahaśivaratri

Crisply   burning   up the sky
Tails   of fire   come to try
Domination.   Lord with hair
Aflame   do you unlock your lair
And summon   death   made at creation
For once   for all   end the nations

Watching seas   of spirit   burning
In your cradle   endless   turning
Whose end no earth can hold   whose mouth
Shrieks forth   always   an unquenched drought
Settle   dear friend   I seek a stern
Unwinking arbitration   an end

Grown-up

When I was a child I'd sometimes lie at night
Awake, and hear my parents talk in bed:
I could make little out of what they said
But I could tell, their stern susurrations light
Today's events to rest. So comforted,
I'd fall asleep, wishing to be a man,
To lie thus in the matrimonial bed,
To talk today away, and make a plan
For tomorrow.

But now that forty years
Have made me half a man at least, my wife
And I exchange good-nights, then fall asleep:
It's surely not because we have no fears
To cherish, or we know we have lived life
One golden day; but that our clay will keep.

To K, Who Said a Poem Ended Weakly

But that is how texts end, my dear,
With neither bangs nor whimpers, but
Some scarce indefinable fear
Which the next word might forget.

So here it is I draw the line
Beneath a trace of thought I thought:
I knew this much, that this was mine,
And ceased before it should be not.

I say this because what I write
Is, once written, become my friend,
And what comes after may, despite
Old friendship, seek another end.

First Infinities: Need

Desperate with knowledge, opened wide by drink,
How I've thrown my need about the houses
I've partied in; how tainting the responses.
How crudely eager to be loved, and how
Vile next day, with J flinging in my face

My sottishness, not allowing me to think,
His poisoned tongue flickering, my vulgar vows
To be good again. I took my chances
And paraded them; and now,
Put out to grass in an accustomed place

I count them one by one. To find a city
Where I have not been foolish: Difficult lies
And truths despicable in their fragility,
Both lack the charm of inadequacy.

First Infinities: Hospital

The doctor's hand was asking what my liver
Meant to do. I thought behind the curtains of
This purpose of my birth, to lie and act
Like one soon to be a corpse. Wayside station
Blues, city living blues, writer's cramp blues.

I had of countless bottles made a river
And discovered its source. Yet one more dropped its love
Into my slow veins. The tiled walls did not in fact
Confine; they wrung from me definition
And made me what I am. Tell me now what use

The pills, the fruit, nurse's disgusted eye
Or glucose, or molasses. No life is short
That at its centre has this clarity.

First Infinities: Drying Out

For I asked myself, What is worth this pain?
And my spirit said: Do not think of Hell
Or hope of Hereafter. Breathing this filth
In a stale room, aching for the fire
To flow in you again—only believe this.

Only ashes clog and clot my veins.
It is in another life that I was well
And time moves like the sea. I spew and spit
The yellow bile. My bones are torn entire.
They look at me and laugh. I am what is.

And what is this I am, in a rude day
Bright with the flame of fever? Spirit replied,
I am the Truth, and the Life, and the Way.

Dvija
to Achhan

When
the dying hour of evening opens its eyes and sees
the lidless hour of night
and shudders, then is engendered, then is
this awe and this secret
this moment that trembles
like dew upon the flower which has not yet opened
this myth
calling the bats out of the violet light.

                    There are bells in the churches,
bells hang in the silence, they are spoken,
speaking of what may only be spoken in this dusk.

                    The echoes of what may become
swell into the violet hour of my time.

I shut my lidless eyes and sit still.

Here
this is the expectation that follows an opening door
and of hesitant footsteps that wait outside my
door

                    In the distance
where the sky stands still and considers us
you, you only

but here are the distant voices trooping out of
cinema halls, forcing the city
to flow into the gutters, the mudfaced houses,
here is the abrupt clap of a muted hand.

In one such hour
I turned my eye to the sky, and my ears
to the call swelling from the thin-pierced minaret
but in my spirit there was
        something else
        something unspoken,
left unsaid: deeds done, battles won
love regained and conquered, the cycles of action
repeating themselves and left incomplete.

Again, I turned my eyes
to where the violet light ebbed between the window bars
and looked for, waited for
my father's ghost, looked for, waited for,
seated on my bed
his legs folded beneath him like the lotus
and his hands shaped in a smile.

He did not question softly why I failed;
instead, looked at my ashtray
and asked me, so you have not yet stopped to smoke?

I did not answer him. How could I answer him?

        He spoke to me
no secrets, but quietly paraphrased

my answers, so that I could not frame
my questions;   he said,
as I walked this way
I saw a woman in her hovel
mourning the death of her man.
                    Her hands like knives,
she clutched the sky to her breast, let it go
and rent the air with manic gestures.
The fierce scent of her clothes muddied the air
and made me, for a moment, think of what I had lost.
But as in the moment of your giving, you are divorced
from the nature of your needs, I forgot these
things I had known from another life
and I spoke to her.
                    Woman, I said,
why do you weep? Is he not luckier than you are,
to escape this wheel? Will you not let him go,
and send with him something that you lived for?

                         But she wailed, and said,
he worked each day in the mill, and now
there is no one to bring home the grain,
sneaking it past the guards in the folds of his cloth
as he used to. I cannot forget
how I would scold him for his drunkenness,
and he would beat me; and later
when the moon was young and hot in the palm fronds
we would share the comfort of the earth
and I would touch him, and hold his shoulder

close, close to me
and the stink of his breath was like honey.
But now he is gone.
                    I said,
Woman, you are to be pitied. But think again.
He was a man, and lived, and now is dead,
he may not be remembered except with tears,
and tears will not preserve the traditions of your house.
He is best forgotten.
                              Then
her eyes grew like stones
        and her tongue darted at me like a snake
and she drove me thence with such words
as I had minded, had I not known her shame.

                              He was silent
Except that the trees stirred outside
at the passing of the wind. He drummed
his fingers lightly on his knee (a gesture
I remembered well) as a man will
when he strives towards the past.
                              He said again,
When I was young and of the old earth,
the old house, I was of the earth
and the fields, and the birds that sang
each morning sang too within my heart.
And I would go each morning to the pool;
my feet knew the earth and the broken tiles
and yesterday's flowers; and the chill red sun

would lie beneath the hills
and wait for the dark spirits within the banyan tree
to end their vigil.
                    I would dive
many times into the clear green water, and took no heed
of bruised shins and fingers. When the water closed
over my head, I heard all the sounds of another world
I was not learned to formulate; and then
I would rise gasping from the water, the air
sounding in my ears like a bell; I would wonder
what I had lost.
                    One such time.
I saw a flower in the crannied steps
that led down into the water, steps made of moss
and the sharp stone beneath which held your toes
and would not let go.
                    I had never seen such a flower.
I cannot properly describe it to you, for in the water
it was dark and absurd from above. I am not sure
even if it was a flower—but something
there was about it—I had never
seen such a flower.
                    It was too deep
to be reached with fingers, and too perilous
to be dived for; and there were water snakes
and tiny creatures with sharp mouths, down
by the water-covered steps. I was afraid
of their poison, and of the stories of my aunts
who spoke sometimes in dreadful whispers
of such flowers as these.

                    I did not try to gain the flower.
Instead, I felt   choked
as if by some presence in the water
reaching out an old and wrinkled hand
covered with moss. I did not stay, I fled.

He laughed. The evening turned to night
He spoke again.
                    Now, I can wish
that I had tried to reach my flower, I feel
there was more to it than I had guessed.
I feel that things—oh, you know what I mean!
—that it would have been different. Even had I drowned
it would have been different.

The first moths of darkness
flitted against the glass; surprised
to see no light where they had been accustomed to light,
they blundered for a while, and ceased.
I was still, but my heart beat within my breast.

My father,
the ghost that had been my father
spoke again, and his voice was like the wind.
                    Son, he said,
son, when my wife died, when your mother
died, I was possessed by a curious guilt.
I felt not grief for her passing—what I believe
I believe, and you are not so young

as not to know what made you.
No, I shed no tears for her dying:
I was not sad because she left me,
I did not complain at her leaving me;
these things are not needed.
                      But I thought,
we have never sat alone together
and linked our fingers; we have not felt
with our eyes what we are to each other
nor looked as one at the evening outside
and thought what it means to us. Oh, all these things
have happened; we have loved
and we have lived together; but always there is
something
something that is denied us
      that will not be
         and if I had her here again with me—
just for a moment, one hour as a man—
                      But no,
even now it may be denied, and even now
I do not grieve that it has passed beyond me
For she is gone, she is not,
              She has ceased to be.
She never was.
She cannot exist because she does not exist.
Perhaps you are not old enough to understand,
but it may be you are, and have felt
the need to remember, and the necessity
of oblivion. I do not regret her loss,
as you will not regret mine. It is better so.

                                          And then
as the coarse-woven mattress pressed its soft
insistent imprint on my thighs, and the clock
dropped its exhausted noises as water
in a dry well,
                  the night outside
                reached with casual fingers in
                and reached into the room,
and kissed with indifferent lips my open eyes,
that I should not remember, that I should not see
and remember what I had seen.
                            With all my heart
I called it to me, and found sweet refuge
in its friendlessness, and called it mother.
I called the night to me, and I was alone.

You, Wystan Auden

Now six feet beneath the air
The Nordic shape of skull is bare
And behind the august frown
Worms have gorged on verb and noun....

The baffling lines that seemed to trace
Maps of care upon his face,
Now nothing between brow and chin
But maggots have tunnelled in....

And the hands whose fingers'-ends
Once touched the keys to common sense
And the truly careless wrist
(Which cherubs have often kissed)

Lie open now without pretence
That they enclose arguments
To shatter prison doors, or shake
The steps of wisdom on the make....

The compassionate eyes that hate
Could not face and grew desperate,
Now bony voids where worlds once turned
In agony at being burned....

The heart that could some pity find
For every shape of human fiend
Now less than dust, because from thence
No spring of friendship does commence....

Of all those works of lust and pain
No mortal fragment can remain
And all that foolishness is past

Yet our lives are still so vast....

And in that vastness since we speak
Strong words of love though we are weak
He cannot know: something survives
The carrion bleaching of our lives.

To Dom

In the light of the day
I wished I was drunker:
Heedless of the way,
Huddled in my bunker,
With rain on the roof,
A good book to hand,
Some 85 proof
And the hell with the land.

But now it is dark
And the song has been sung.
The vision is stark
Of when I was young
And would dream of the lines
I was meant to write,
The complex designs,
All wise and all bright.

You are to me now
A god in excess.
I wonder at how
You're still able to bless.
If something to give
Is all the prayer,
Look at me and live,
Poet and sayer.

My liver is rotted,
Cancerous my tongue.
My thoughts are all clotted,
I am no longer young.
But still I can make—
Because you give—
From deed and mistake
One reason to live.

Half-life

Half a lifetime ago
    We last met
And have swept our failings, since,
    Under the carpet.

If we should meet again, now,
    Whom will you blame
For parting, or shall I play
    The silly game

Of trying to remember
    Why we failed?
Your poems that I wrote then
    Have not gone stale:

Radium decays
    A bit at a time;

Your poems have burned away
    Line by half-line.

The words that smouldered then
    Smoulder still
Where, half a lifetime ago,
    You wished them well.

Profit

A Little Better

A little water trickled down a little pipe
Left leaning by the wall when the roofers
Had laid the guttering. It went along
The earth, asking until it was needed.
                            Now
There is a little green thing there, hardly
A plant, come of a seed which lay in wait,
And whether it has leaves or feathers or
Wings, I must wait to discover.
                              It is
Not a green I care for: not a green I use
In crayon, or in cloth: too rich, too loud
With treasure, too pleased with itself.
                             How
They'd laugh, the harvesters outside
In the fields damp with paddy, their fingers
Clutching goodness, if I showed them such a yield!
The land is rank with rice this year, the price
Is down.
             And so this little greenling sits
In the sun, satisfied with itself,

Whatever it is.
            Whatever it is,
It cannot make things as they are any worse,
And nobody is the poorer for its pleasure.

Essay in Capitalism

Down, down the Shanty Road our bodies go
Bag in hand, searching for the choicest fish
Or potatoes, or melons—while we who know
There will never be so succulent a dish

Again as that my smiling mother cooked
On Sunday afternoons—we sit inside the car,
Pale hands on the wheel, and if anyone looked
We would not be there. We are afar

Buying vegetables down the Shanty Road.
...And now if I should do like that bearded guy
Who rawhide whip in hand subdued the crowd,
Lashing the corrupt flesh till it ceased to cry

'Four for eight!' or 'Come here, I give you more!'
—Then I would wait for signs among the fish
Telling me, Summon now anger from your store
And you'll be unselfconscious as you wish.

Until then, pale hands upon the wheel
I sit while my body goes forth to buy
Leaving behind whatever makes me feel
The aches of beggars who affectedly sigh

About my windows. Now I let in the clutch
And leave the Shanty Road, and the beggars know
Although I am not immune to their touch
I am that beardless guy who makes the market go.

No Fallacy Is Pathetic

Above, the sentimental sky is matching colours.
I know it well by now. Picking on someone below,
If no human a dog then or a cow, the bent
Of a ruining wall, a bush with thorns and flowers,
A tree (single for preference). Mood for mood

The sky changes: black for anger, dull brown
With dust and thirst, a slow western crimson
For the dying-out of passion, soft beddable blue
In comfort and carelessness, or as now
Like the deep sea bringing back forgotten things.

It never can resist a touch of the dramatic,
Never be itself: no man can be miserable but
It too must let fall two giant tears. The clouds

Serve perhaps to hide behind when it has to laugh.
—Blush, then, I think I touched a nerve that time.

Only at night can I bear to look at it,
More or less inhuman, unfamiliar as the womb
—Although even then with assorted jewels it tries
To look as if it had a date. Whoever made it
Thought it very important to condescend to us.

Meeting a Translator

We drove to the airport in a solitary rain,
Exchanging languages as competing fleets
Divided the sky. After I had checked in
We sat in the bar; we drank amicably,
We had an argument, and were friends once more.
We shook hands when we parted. Later, when
The plane flew over the suburb where he lives
He hurled my silence up to me again.

The Fly in the Ointment
(on seeing a worm crawl out from my notebook)

This maggot from among my poems poked its head,
Its shiny head of bruised black, trembled stiffly,

Hesitating as I hesitated
To plunge the penpoint in and rid my rhyme
Of this reminder of its predestined time.

Do I know what insincere word I wrote
Caused this evil to hatch here, assuming
Property in the fabric of my thought?
Not exactly; but poets never can guess
What it is makes their magic to grow less.

The poetry's not only in the form:
I know some aberration of my mind
Has taken root here and produced this worm.
One sick neuron will lay the sordid curse
Of unsuccess on all my meagre verse.

But—I explain why I hesitate—
Should I kill this misbegotten creature if
It really does reflect my creative state?
Truth is beauty, just like the man said,
So I must preserve truth if I'm to be read.

Therefore I will research each youthful page,
Undoing my folly. Yet take comfort, for
This apparition's only in the larval stage
And if I work well, in my astonished eye
It will grow wings and appear a butterfly.

Names

I don't believe in fancy names.
Fancy names come close to touch
Yet slip away, and soon play games
With my medulla. I don't like them much,

But am forced to contend daily
With names skirting sanity's edge
Which then skip alongside gaily
Telling me Acceptance, that's our pledge.

Why should U2, iPod live?
Our language grasps for tenuous
Moments where it can survive,
Its clasp sensitive, but ingenuous.

What is it to make a name?
I catch as catch can, but insist
That every sense give to my gain.
Does Paris Hilton live? Must will.i.am exist?

Making Tea

What a difference a pinch of tea-leaf makes
Twinkling on the surface of the water,
Bronzing it, burnishing it, turning it gold.

And in the cup, a lake of such enchantment:
Merry at the edges, brimful with laughter,
Wearing its meniscus like a crown.
                                        Go on,
Drink it: There is nothing after this
But a bitterness in the mouth.

And in the cup,
Some say, the pattern of your life is drawn
If you have the nerve to turn it upside down.

Pills

Some pills are sugar-coated.
                            And some are not.
Some are encapsulated in gelatine
And some are not.
                    Those that are handed out
For ailments of the mind, I have realized,
Are always *au naturel*.
                        Why must this be so?
Why cannot the pill-makers disguise them, too,

Behind milk and honey?
                    Is it so that we,
Carrying our bitterness with us always
Like a mask behind a mask, should know
What it is to be unmasked—we should be told
This is the bitter taste we give to a sweet world
And learn to sugar coat ourselves like the rest?

―――――

Making Coffee

I measure decoction into a cup,
Add milk and water, pour the whole into
A suitable cauldron, and place it
On the stove.
              Some stoves are born to make trouble,
But this one clicks sweetly into flame.

Now I can stand and look at greenness
Outside the window, now I can forget
To forget, until it's time to turn down the flame.
There is something in the making of coffee
That dulls the moral sense.
                          I spoon in sugar
And sip that first sip against which it is vain
To argue.
         Not strong enough.
                            I must add
Some instant powder, which I loathe, or spoon in

Some more decoction, which will make it cold.

This is not how the masters advocate
The making of coffee, but I have succeeded
In taking seven thinking minutes off my life.

Lint

Those who sweep beneath beds know the smell of lint.
It is something like musk, murmuring of age
And wickedness: something less than ashes, more than
    dust.
Lighter than the air which wafts above the bed,
Yet heavy as that which weighs upon your head at night
When you want sleep and it will not come.
                                              Lint is light
Captured in windows, kept captive against the dark:
It is all of yesterday that we wished to forget,
Creeping silently back when we thought it was gone.

Lint is power, wicked only in its weakness. Lock
It in cupboards and it triumphs; sweep it aside
And it owns no master.
                              The smell of lint is thus
The smell of waking to the very ill, who need
No compassion, but it smothers them. Yet those
Who sweep beneath beds are also sometimes wise,

And they know enough to leave the lint alone.

Those Blind from Birth

Those blind from birth know they have eyes
Because they do not know what darkness is
Different from the kingdom where they dwell,
Thinking that this is all. Those blind from birth
Can smell the redness of a rose, can hear
The muted silver of a flute, and touch
Granite's own grey. Those blind from birth can feel
Pity in others like a black shroud pressed
Upon their eyes. Their eyes are inward-looking, so
Why should they know the pangs of earth's
Each dawn, or mourn when doomed lives end?
Those blind from birth have sometimes their
Own particular reason not to see:
It is not a reason you or I require.

These Were My Homes

These were my homes then, though I did not know:
The swell of the womb, and a mother's long breast
And the small peace of a children's house;
The blankets of my bed, and the night's rest

Beneath, and then the waking to sweet air.

These were my homes, though they did not know me
The worn cool green of my father's lands,
Older than battle; the wars that won them;
The moments lingering, for each was planned
And I only had to reach out to sweet air.

Then these are the homes that I will know yet:
One book to live in, one honest page,
One face to meet at dawn and noon and night,
One storm to soothe, one oblivion, one stage,
One bed in which to breathe my last of air.

At last, the homes made on other roads:
But were these mine to know, mine to be told,
I should not tell lest they should become mine.

Wet Dream

Last night there were ghosts around my bed,
I didn't dream it. Today I saw their traces
In the weave of the bedsheet near my head:
Tracks leading to unrecognized places,
Confused on purpose and seemingly lost.
I did not follow them in sleep. Night has lost its fears,
And their call could not rouse me. They paused
At my stillness, and went away.

It's many years
Since they last came. Did they recognize the child
Who hid from darkness because it was not in him?
I wonder. Now there's enough that is wild
Within me, their spells are powerless and dim.

This morning I watched my mother make the bed.
She sniffed at the sheet. 'Spirits' was all she said.

———

On First Looking into Whitman's Humour

A child said to me: What is grass? and I replied,
It is a weed, not good for much; but if you
Pick some carefully, and dry it several days
In the sun; and you lovingly pack it
Into a ceremonial pipe—
                    No, he interrupted,
Not that grass! The green grass—do you perhaps
Think it to be the uncut hair of graves?
So I threw a book at him and went on smoking.

———

Summer Triangle

You know, while I lie here in bed and write
Far above my head the stars are playing out
Their autumnal dance.

                      The rains are over
(They may have other plans) and yesterday
From the terrace I caught a glimpse of Swan
And Lyre and Eagle.

                    Such pure light was not
Invented just for us to rejoice by, I'm sure,
But we had been friends for many years.

            So as I play with toys, with pen and book
In bed, in the stars' wakes drift to what strange ends
What strange bedfellows.

                          Almost, in the night,
They break their bounds and hover near. They range
The blackness, always searching, it seems now
In my own blackness, for what is over
And can be rewritten only in my book.

The Rain Is Pouring down Again

The rain is pouring down again, and all
The grass is overjoyed. Naturally it knows
Nothing of the jaws that clomp in half
Its pride, the guileful steel that cuts
In two its prime. Why should it grow
Thinking these thoughts? Its seeds scatter
Where its murderers will, and in small days
To come, will sprout again.
                             We who keep our heads
And stunt our hopes, we also know something
That grass has glimmerings of: Of suns gone
Without goodbyes, of parched earth and wayward winds
Which do not wait.
                          And yet our proud roots clutch
At tenuous soil, that holds our lives together
And is willing to be divided at a touch.

A Gift of Tongues

If I were a young man, I should be a thief:
I should steal from those possessed of gifts beyond belief.
Somewhere I'd find a simpler mind, somewhere a sharper pen,
I'd find the gifts I find I've lost between this now and then.
From one a livelier liver, from one unblackened lungs—
But most of all, from where it fall, I'd filch the gift of tongues.

All languages approach sages with familiar ease;
My halting mouth they tiptoe to as if it bears disease.
I grant myself a turn for scripts and signs and silly things
But O the bird of many hues within me never sings.
I can comment on many climes under their many suns
But scarce six suns have ever shone 'neath which I made a pun.

The land where I was born has tendered loving words to me:
A score and more of wonders burn here between sea and sea.
What root to hold, what stem shall bear my inward-turning guile,
What branches wait for one whose wits will not be prehensile?
This language which I wage will take me all one life to learn:
One birth, one death, one betweenness, one piety to discern.

God grant me hope again; God grant a milder manner yet;
God grant I remember before I begin to forget;
God grant the wishes that I wished be unwished ere they fail;
God grant my soul may never be on envy's spear impaled;
God grant me expectation, long after I am young;
God grant me naught—except what's wrought with magic of the tongues.

———

Neighbours

Sunita Williams is in India now
And on a TV show they asked her if
She'd like to visit Mars.
                      Yeah, sure, she said.
The god of war is straying near the sun,
Or I'd step out tonight and ask him if
He would like Ms Williams to visit him.

Even a lady should ask a gentleman.

Have we become such boors? Are all these worlds
There simply for our taking? Are we so bored
By life on earth? When Tereshkova
Spent a day in space, it thrilled us more
Than when Sunita stayed up there six months.

Those glittering worlds, those gleaming, glittering worlds
Are so familiar, we think of them
As just across the street.
                      Our Father's house
Has its many mansions, and there surely
We shall live as neighbours are meant to do:
Windows will need no curtains, doors no locks
And we no questions.
                      Star requires of star
Nothing but being: In some world to come
Each house shall be only the threshold of the next.

The Corporate Poet

Brightness fails from the air.
Queens have died young and fair.
Dust hath closed Helens eye.

                                              Nashe

Briefly his pen slithers among
Pieces of language, sorting and emending,
Telling right from wrong.

It is poetry that he's making—
The highest art of all, transforming truths
From insistent dreams to his harsh waking.

His ear tells the trueness of ideals and abstractions,
His voice is the voice of peoples, raised in hope,
Of Solemn Moments and Centenary Celebrations.

Briefly his pen tells right from wrong,
Very briefly—he must finish by seven
And turn then to refining the words of a song

For a Bombay film. His Ongoing Venture
(To be declaimed in London at the Festival of India)
Must delay his new book, which is critical of Culture;

Impatient with these trivialities, he cannot devise
A new rhyme for 'pyaar'; Art, unfortunately,
Is subject to the restrictions on private enterprise

But he plans to attack this in a speech he will deliver
At the capital's Literary Festival next week
Which will make the Ministry's mandarins quiver—

Quoting from Foucault, he will demonstrate
How Poetry may prosper on Government funds
And uphold the example of the Soviet State...

Meanwhile, there's the sher to be written still
For Hindustan Steel: It will be preserved in marble
At the theatre complex they propose to build—

Oh, if he can only find the time!
Tonight in bed he will Free Associate
For five or ten minutes; out of one meaningful rhyme

He will fashion a poem short, clever, pithy
For tomorrow's meeting with fifty college girls
Who'll find him remarkably urbane and witty.

If FA fails there's always the oration
On Language as an Ethic, from the Akademi's fête:
He can render that without preparation.

———

A Town Like Ali's

It is a town somewhat like Ali's, the railway runs as ever
By dirty backsides of palaces, where the poor folk shiver
Early mornings in the winter, perched atop the gutters
Losing on what little's entered, and the red flags flutter
Atop their shacks, old tin and sacks, their incurious gazes
Seeing wheels turn within wheels, and not passengers' faces.

In this town which is like Ali's, the cinema houses brightly
Flicker neon, swallow, release mortality nightly.
Bodies come and bodies go, the streetlamps count the traffic;
When Ali wakes from dreams he knows a vision most fantastic:
Each night after tears and laughter, with concrete heart and
   loins
The city bears more concrete lairs, and each to each it joins.

Ali's moved from town to town, each the other's mirror:
What cannot go up must go down, and falling has its terrors.
He knows the old temples and mosques, where sometimes from
   danger
He creeps to hide, and never asks the ineffable stranger
To whom they pray O every day, what cities lie before him,
What anxious trade his parents made, what boxes wait to store
   him.

When Ali was a little boy, his town fit snug around him;
Now strange perils and stranger joys have taken it beyond him.
On the pavements, in the sewers, he smells the smell of money:
The notes are only gay deceivers, the coins stick like honey.

He lives between mighty and mean, kings' avenues and galis,
And everywhere there is a snare which is a town like Ali's.

Shame and Renown

The first line is from Hafiz

If you call me shamed, then shame is my renown
Which winds its web around the deaths of kings
But, blind to other earthly happenings,
Ignores him destined not for gibbet nor crown.
Thieves rejoice in their fingers, women who
Live by pleasing men (as most women do)
Pride themselves on false shame, and merchants still
Win more renown the more they pad the bill.
Poets sell their words, and their own worth
Is measured not in hearts bought but copies sold.
Then why should accident of breed or birth
Prevent my doing what was not foretold?
Shame cannot speak unless it cheats the frown
The world wears, with the gaudy robe renown.

NEW POEMS

Good Friday
First published in the Wailing Wall Street Journal

That day I'd smoothed my pitch and on my mat had spread
The little things by which I have earned my daily bread
These fifteen years and more: There were perfumes of Arabia
(Which I make up by the score with the assistance of Flavia,
The Praefect's wife's handmaiden), and purple dye from Tyre
And silks and such from Sidon which—so you won't call me liar—
Were strictly speaking made at home. But many and various,
When being Romans under Rome, and counting each denarius,
Are the shifts a prudent man must make. As I say we did it,
Each merchant had his little stake, the Temple had the credit.

Some sold oils from Africa and some goats from Galilee,
Some were scroll-holder makers and some cried out lustily
Their copies of the Torah. Some changed money, some lent,
Some polished old menorahs, some were straight, some bent.
And the devout came amply, some silent, some abuzz
To Eloi in his Temple. It was a normal day for us.

Then suddenly sprang from nowhere a muscular young fellow,
Ice-cold angry was his stare, his voice was a bull's bellow.
I thought first he was simple, for this is what he said:
'This is my father's temple'—his father's? God forbid!
'This is my Father's House, and you have made it a den of
  robbers!'

(Now this is simply not true, and not nice to say to neighbours.)
'This was of old a house of prayer: you buy and sell and cheat here!
'Gehenna knows you: Go back there!' and as if it was his métier
He seized a knout and whirled it about and made it taste our flesh;
With the wild shout, 'Get out! Get out!' he cleansed the yard
    afresh.

He girded up his loins and he swore most unseemly;
He upset the stacks of coins and he let the doves go free.
Then heard I no Hosannas, for our weekly trade was spoiled,
And I glimpsed upstairs old Annas as he bit his beard and boiled.
We cowered and were driven in manner most barbarous;
O Eloi in his Heaven! It was a terrible day for us.

Now it is the Pesah. The angel's sword has spared,
(And it was the lesser of the evils at which we stared.)
That sword will never fail us, for it strikes those who blaspheme
—The one disease which ails us—in our own Jerusalem.
We've been mocked and flayed for faith and trade, stinted by
    war and by peace;
But we have stayed so long as we've prayed at the Holy of Holies.
It's an ill wind blows no profit: Now with perfumes of Arabia
I stock for believers to scoff at tokens of the 'Saviour'.
Five days ago we made a loss, but clever is Caiaphas.
O bleeding Christ upon the Cross! What a jolly day for us.

Billennium

Over time, the very mountains changed, dwindled
Into deserts, and new mountains grew snow elsewhere.
The great shapes of land shifted, made oceans
Of lakes; the seas themselves became pools and puddles
And then deserts. All this happened, over time.

Then so slowly we had not perceived it, green
Touched the shores of land, tinged the ocean edges
And spread and spread, and coloured all the planet
With profusion. We had waked and slept
And waked again to see these changes, over time.

There was movement when next we looked, but we had
To look very closely. We saw the bubbles
Infinitely small, in the seas; the slow stretching
Later, of limbs on land. Pseudopods, tentacles
In turn levered life to dominion—over time.

We saw it was our time to go down then
And give more than attention. With great patience,
Great care not to change what had itself begun
To change, we moved and manipulated and at last
Seeded the seeds which would succeed: over time.

Now this was all long ago, in history-less time
For that planet. Now, over time—we seeded well—
The seeds we planted must have grown great roots and realms,
Must know by now what it is to be great. So now
We are returning, to see what has become of Man.

The Sunday Mystery Show

He is like a magician who can repeat
His one trick each week, and no one can see
Just how he does it. It's the same trick, too:
How boring for anyone who doesn't believe
It's magic.
               Sister Maggie, Cousin Teresa,
Do you lower your eyes to show devotion,
Or do you believe because you're not allowed
To see?
        It's no great matter;
To us who are let to watch both you and him,
There's still some magic in it. With bread
That's tasteless and with unfermented wine,
Father Ralph still makes our hairs to stand on end.

To Vivekananda, Jr

Narendra, when the gods come calling
    Will you render strict account
Of all the times you might have fallen
    Off your high and mighty mount?

You perceive paths we've not seen yet;
    Still, the elephant is a beast
Who does not, will not, cannot forget
    Fright nor favour, fret nor feast.

The pachyderm on which you're perching
    Is a thousand million strong;
Left and right alternate lurching,
    Straight the road it moves along.

When the gods come calling, Naren,
    Look behind and you will see
Where you thought you were you aren't,
    What you made is still to be.

The sun is westing, but the east
    Is just as bright as all you feared:
What inglorious god has seized
    This time to creep up on your rear?

Though the mind is strong, determined,
    And the chest be five feet round,
Still the pachyderm is thin-skinned,
    Fifteen men make that funereal sound.

You gaze before with steel-rimmed eyes,
    Destiny seems to meet your gaze:
But what power in your glasses vies
    With Gandhi's for a nation's praise?

The bands sing out the ballots' count,
    The voters vote and depart hence.
From up there, do you think you can count
    On a billion to display sense?

Easily you disdain, easy
    Rest the laurels round your biceps;
When you've fallen off the beastie,
    Will you so easily rise up?

But put these thoughts aside of falling,
    Perched so smugly in your howdah:
Until that day the gods come calling,
    Let the hosannas sound louder.

The democrickest custom, Naren,
    Is the gift of easy dreaming.
A dictator's right is to arrange
    The dreams which are coming teeming.

Then let the salute royal ring out,
    The elephant raise his trunk and bawl,
Let the crowds ecstatic sing out,
    'We have all we needed, all!'

Schrödinger's Cat

Spare a thought for pretty puss,
    Imprisoned in a box,
Wondering what's all the fuss
    With bearded men and clocks.

What's her conception of Time
    Whose breakfast, lunch and tea
May come with reason or with rhyme
    But were not—they will be.

All the hours spent in slumber
    Flashed between milk and fish
Yet aeons without number
    Lie in an empty dish.

When the deadly rays have ceased,
    When this has become that,
Does it matter to the deceased
    Just who, and when, said 'Scat'?

The Temple

'What is this house, so like a cave
    With walls of granite and moss?'

'Here is the church, here is the nave,
    Coming to worship are those
Who leave all thought, all pretence behind
    And beg their hearts to be still.
They are not sure of what they may find
    But only are sure that they will.'

'Then who is the god that can command
    Such obedience from men,
Whence comes this power which can withstand
    The bloody wilfulness of men?'

'There is no god here, only a house
    They have come to since Time began.
There is no church here, only a space,
    No pillars, no lintel, no span,
Only somewhere they have brought their vows
    And worship because they can.'

Lent

It is easy to die for saving of the world.
Can you die for a flower which withers, uncurled
Too early from bud? For a fledgeling new spilt
From the nest which its parents so carefully built?
Can you die praying, face proper and prim
When you are impaled at a tyrant's whim?
Can you die even for the sake of your twin
Who ruined his life and his liver with gin?

For forty days now we do penance for one
Who died for us, say the priests, who was God's son.
We sustain ourselves with fish and with chips,
Remembering him who was sustained with whips.
And I think he must think it is very strange
That he thought by his thoughts anything could change.

Cophetua

She came to church, but turned away
From where we watched within the hall
And seating herself, bent to pray
To the Lady on the wall.

Her shoulders bowed, and soon they shook
And soft though her sobs in the vast
Distance to us, yet they took
Some of the burden of the Mass.

We could not ask, but silent made
Our own communion, and stole
Away from grief which could not stay
Apart from us, wanting the whole.

We looked up to the altar too
Wondering how the Christos slept
His naked sleep; yet hoped, or knew
All the while, that Jesus wept.

For the Tibetan New Year

Who knows what's happening in Tibet now
As the machine-guns settle beneath the snow
Which is marked by the slow hoofbeats of yaks
Who plod on weighed down by soldiers' packs
And the soldier lights a dreary cigarette
Longing for the cold to let him forget.

Who knows what's happening in Tibet now?
Does he sit in the city of a thousand years
Or in a timbered hut on Shimla's hills?
Does he dream of dominion until it fills
His heart with the sharp-angled, insolent fear
That someone else knows all about Tibet now?

The Evidence of My Senses

Just Talk

If I breathe deep with my eyes closed, and my hands
Held just so on my knees, the fingers shaped
In frozen dance, and direct the indrawn breath
Just so, I'm told I may cause to affirm
Any organ I choose.
            So I choose my tongue,
Will it to detect poison, to dissolve
The detritus of uncountable smokes,
To flow correctly in speech, and above all
I will it to be still.
            If I had six tongues
And each loved one language, I would yet
Will each separate one to stay from speech.

The lover most fully understands his love
In absence, sleep without comfort of touch
—Loving without love, losing without loss,
Confinement while free, possessed of grace
While motionless—
            In all that is devout,
Is not there an unspeakable place.

Integument

Hold me tight, my skin, I fear you may burst
Before your time with ripeness, and show the world
My red heart of anger. Hold me tight, I pray,
That I may not be compelled to face the worst
With worser still. What, will this blood be shed
From mere longing, saying what cannot be said?

Yet burst if you will, for I well know
Inside, that inside is another wall
Which will hold off anything that may call
For your destruction. That shield's blazons show
Like a mirror, the vitals of compassion.
It can never burst in such a fashion.
A second skin is something more than skin.

Hear, Hear

My ears are shells where sings the sea.
Canals run from them to the
Accepting brain, and each sound makes
A cell for the moment it takes.

When stillness sounds, how will I know?
The sea's in spate, will remain so.
I want surcease from sounding seas,
Shell-shocked by storm, I war for peace.

One day the sound will cease, and then
I will be as a child again.
And to one voice I'll turn my ears:
Speak now, for Thy servant hears.

Smell of Things to Come

A nose is a nose is a nose. Who knows
Those fibres of smell better than I? The scent
Of a book that grows on me, of a rose
Withered by fondling, of newsprint, of drink
Untasted but soon to be consumed, of course
I know them all and know too the gross
Odours of unwashed flesh, of dirt
Shed or retained by skin, and I know almost
The scent of love, because sometimes it flows
Between breast and breast, and my nose
Has nestled there.
           When blows the wind above
My senses, I have smelled the clouds grow
Against the sky. One scent remains to know,
The last breath I shall ever take as I.

An Eye for an Eye

Now that I wear glasses, I feel the urge
To close my eyes more often. What burden
It is to see and keep on seeing.
When I shut my eyes, I hear and smell and touch
Things I'll never see. A blind man misses
Little beauty, a blind woman none.
I know now I can smell light, hear light
And touch the sun's rays as they fall upon
My face. Were this blackness granted me
For ever, I should still know the grace
Of light.
    But while I breathe I know I never shall
Lose this sight, having known it; it makes me sad
To think I lose never having known loss.

All Cock

He's a fine rooster, this gallant who struts
Around the yard. Russet, black and green
Are his heraldry, he is all male and
Arrogance.   In his abundant harem
Is a speckled hen, as plump as he is,
Black and white and with a dainty comb.
She is choosy: She lets him mount her
And then squawks and scuttles off, leaving him
To flap his wings foolishly and cry
His foolish challenge to the earth and sky
Like any husband.   Behind them follows
A younger male, leaner, meaner, muscled
And determined in every feather, watching,
Making notes, learning.   Birds of a feather
They say, flock together: It's not for love
But that they are accustomed to being fools
Only with their own kind. Another species
Might find a fault, it's only bestial nature.

What I see is a good dinner for eight.

Familial

One Gift My Father Gave Me

One gift my father gave me: That was anger.
A stirring in the blood. Between the ears
A drum. Smoke filled my eyes. I scented
Tears and the blood of ancestral ghosts,
Preserved in the teak beams of my father's house.

Another gift he gave, and that was love
Of words. How they come together, make
A song. I can only sing for love. I am
Speechless with song, the Sirens never made
Such music as I have heard within my head.

Let me now, O Muse, marry these two gifts
My father gave, let me unrepentant
Burden my words with anger they cannot bear.

My Father's Hand

My father was such a superman,
He made look easy such difficult things.
It is no easy task to beat a child, yet
He could do it.
           When his hand landed on my cheek
It made a sound like doom that tore my ears,
I thought my heart would burst. How will I forget
The tears, the shame? My eyes sting again,
Feeling, remembering.
                  What love and caring
We carry each of us and mean to share
Always tomorrow, or in a better world
More wisely made than this, tomorrow
Or perhaps yesterday; what words we have
To soothe hurts, what all, what all to give
And when we give it is with empty hand.

My Mother Would Not

My mother would not kiss nor curse
After we reached a certain age:
She was there like India asking
Nothing but faith.
         Now she is grey
I wonder where that mother is
Who I thought knew me complete

But knows only how easily
From my face the lies I tell
And never searches to know more.

Where is she gone? My memories say
This is the same mother who held
That all that I could say was true.

The secret in the mother's breast
Is what only a child might know
Who without kiss or caress
Prepares to show its face above.

Some secret within India is
No one has found nor searches for
Which will not kiss which will not curse
And hangs from itself such a lie
I never will know completely.

———

On Vishu

My father had a chest at home he filled
With all the old years. Each day done, he dipped
His mind in each gone hour; and then he sipped
Its poison again, all that he'd been willed
To do.
    One day, too young to know, I sneaked
A look, and it was all dry, all that he would

Have done had the world been great and good
Was missing. So much of lostness it reeked,
His life was worse than living.
                 Now I have lived
These fifty years to tarnish what he prized:
His chest of years by rust is held and seized
And the days like handsome black have dropped
From his head. His days were never mine; he stopped
Belief before he knew what he believed.

Frost in Summer

To return to a familiar place
Is so familiar, I must have done
It thirty thousand times at least. The fun
Is all gone out of it; each familiar face
(But one) glares hatefully at my return
And only the sticks and stones and trees
Look on with a compassion which does not free
My bones from old hurts. They think it does not burn
Me to be back? But being back at home
Means not only that they have to take me in.
They must want me. Wherever I have been,
Wherever mind and body have been made to roam,
I've felt at ease in that strangeness which ends
In the familiarity of a friend.

Calypso to Odysseus

If you are not interested in what I have to say,
Let my words fall anyway, like mermaids' voices
In the background, hushing you, but not saying
Anything you may understand. We are here to stay,
You and I, all day and days until the night closes
My song, and your unhearing. If you will be praying
Always for some far sail on the brittle horizon
Why then I will still pray for windless calm; let the gods
(Who, really, care nothing) decide what to send.
You hear cruel warders' voices in your prison;
I see a hero who will not accept. What are the odds,
My hero, fighting loneliness when you have found a
    friend?
On far shores, battle rages; on a far shore your wife
Sits weaving, unweaving, and is content with life.

Duck Poems

Buoyancy

Ducks have, in water, a feeling that they are
Not quite all there. That's why they keep looking down
To see if their nether parts are still of the same
Feather, that they're still together.
                        I too, sometimes
Catch myself looking down to see if my feet
Are still on earth.
            And so when I look up
I return where I belong, after long separation.

Original Sin

Ducks have, in water, all they really
Need, food and drink and exercise
And a tight refuge. Strange to think
They only cannot lay their eggs there
But must land.
        Why would any sane creature
Forsake all amniotic contentment

For these dry and barren bits of earth?
Why did our mothers' mothers climb
Out of the ocean?
      Perhaps there is
In all of us, some primeval notion
That suffering is preferable to bliss.

Double Bill

Ducks have, in water—but only clear water
And in good light—a kind of double life.
The webs vanish, and they are doubly there
Upside down, beaks and ducks' eyes.
                      Only they
When they look down can see both halves,
The webbed and the unwebbed.
                        A duck
Maybe thinks she has reason to hide
What she does with her feet. She must float
For no one must know she can walk on water.

Mach Duck

Ducks have, in water, another medium
To communicate in. Do they know that sound
Travels faster down there, and speak as quickly

As they think, or do they simply blow bubbles
And look silly?
                    I should like to know, but
Water is another medium for me, too,
And if I stooped and immersed my head
I should think of something else entirely,
Probably having nothing to do with ducks.

L'après-midi d'un Canard

Ducks have, in water, a visible class
And grace they completely lack on land.
Do they feel it, to be hypocrites,
To shrug off the clumsy Quasimodo walk
And slip noiselessly into Nijinsky?

Well, hardly Nijinsky; but how easily
They lure the viewer into hyperbole
Just by stepping off, as if they did not know
That turbid, weed-choked pond contained
All they had forgotten of their fate.

Shanghai Girls

O Shanghai girls have swinging legs and do not shame to show them.
Where I come from the girls just haven't had the time to grow them.
They are encased from birth in sheaths of cotton or of nylon,
But here they just go on and on like pylon after pylon.
So proud they stand, so close to hand, how I long to touch—
But errant males in China's jails do not rejoice too much.

Take 2

If I could be a band upon that thigh, to touch that cheek,
It's all I'd ask, and just the asking makes me grow so weak.
I am a band—a hussy-band—and have a role to play,
So stand afar and adore all the legs across the way.
We husbands must, till we are dust, admire only the silk
Of household flesh, and never press any of foreign ilk.

Take 3

But Shanghai's girls have happy hips, and thighs and calves and toesies.
When I go home my memories will all be tinged with roses.
And I will urge the Indian girls to shake off ancient fashions

And stride along the pavements with the most innocent passion.
But then, alas, we Indian men, our hands are sharp and surly,
And errant males from India's jails are released far too early.

The Shopping Mall

The mansion was built of good stone, a stone
Not quarried nowadays: massive and grey,
It yet lent its strength to a manufacture
That was light and graceful.
      It was but
A century old, and for all its light and grace
It had to come down, for in its place
Was to come a shopping mall, shining, spacious,
Its columns decked with names known the world over;
Its corridors alive to the fall, every day,
Of a million excited feet. What to say?
Progress has its price.
      So they razed the palace
To build another in its stead. And then below
Its foundations, they saw the light spires
Of another, older building.
      At once they called
The archaeologists, who dug a thousand days
And uncovered beneath the vanished palace
A shining spacious building, just the same
In every detail, as the proposed shopping mall.

Hand

Lakshmi resides in my fingers,
Goes the old Sanskrit good-saying,
Saraswati is in my fist
    And Krishna in the palm of my hand.

Perhaps he's still there; perhaps lingers
From my boyhood, from when I was praying,
From when I was one counted blessed,
    Perhaps he's there in the palm of my hand.

Of good fortune most of the bringers
Have deserted me—is he still staying,
Is he making a little list
    Of all the lines in the palm of my hand?

Morning Walk

Walking—at so many metres a minute—
Walking past the park and everything in it,
The fat ladies walking to work off their fat,
The young ladies walking only so that
They may be fit to be seen; walking away
From the *Delonix Regea* (not yet in bloom),
Walking to find a place where there's room
For the thoughts which have metastasized all day
To escape or be healed—walking through shade
And the remnants of sun, walking to blow
Up and be done, or to gradually fade
Into the road—but it forever flows
Even farther than thought, and who can be healed
Within whom such knowledge is concealed?

www.ingramcontent.com/pod-product-compliance
Lightning Source LLC
Chambersburg PA
CBHW051118230426
43667CB00014B/2637